What others are saying about *Celebrating Whittier*

"Compiled with imagination and affection, Pamela Fenner's *Celebrating Whittier* is a gala collection of newspaper clippings, photographs, and delightful tributes that, taken together, not only recreates the Whittier Centennial of 1907 but re-introduces us to the beloved Quaker poet and abolitionist who stood tall in tumultuous times and still casts a long, heroic shadow.

—Brenda Wineapple, Editor
John Greenleaf Whittier: Selected Poems
Library of America

"…such a beautiful book—your photo reproductions alone make it worthwhile. You have done yourself proud and made this, I think, the gem of the Whittier Bicentennial. I am grateful for your work and welcome you to the rank of Whittier scholar. The book, in effect, is a presentation of Whittier in his age and by those who knew him."

—John "Ben" Pickard, Co-author
Whittier and Whittierland: Portrait of a Poet and His World
Retired Professor of English, University of Florida
and great-grandnephew of John Greenleaf Whittier

"Makes available Whittier materials that were previously accessible only to the few. Most importantly, Fenner's work affirms and emphasizes the center of Whittier's calling: he served as the conscience of his nation regarding the horrific practice of slavery, and he did so at a time when conscience was that nation's greatest need. Students of Whittier—along with scholars of nineteenth-century poetry and society—owe her their thanks."

—William Joliffe, Editor
The Poetry of John Greenleaf Whittier: A Readers' Edition
Professor of English, George Fox University
Newberg, OR

"I'm impressed in so many ways—with your own dedication in digging out the details of various JGW Centennial celebrations and the extent to which the details of those observances have been presented.

The fact that so many people, organizations and institutions over so broad a span of territory took time to recall and commemorate Whittier's life and work speaks volumes for his impact upon the minds and hearts of Americans back in 1907. I find it difficult to think of any contemporary poet, or author of any sort, whose stature is such as to call forth a region-wide or a nation-wide celebration of the centennial of his/her birth."

—*Ron Kley, Consultant*
Museum Resource Associates
Hallowell, ME

"Pam Fenner's enthusiasm for the life and works of John Greenleaf Whittier is beautifully realized in *Celebrating Whittier: America's 1907 Centennial*. This book is a fine addition to the Whittier historical and literary legacy."

Joseph Dmobowski, Special Collections Librarian
Wardman Library, Whittier College
Whittier, CA

"This collection of materials from the Whittier Centennial will demonstrate to the public what an important figure Whittier was to the country. His work as an abolitionist and poet touched the American heart and psyche and solidified the values of home and country. Ms. Fenner recognized these attributes and through her editorial work has again memorialized Whittier."

—*Janet Heller Howell, President 2006-2008*
Whittier Home Association

"*Celebrating Whittier* is a delightful evocation of a place and time when communities celebrated poets and radical reformers."

— *Thomas D. Hamm, Archivist*
Professor of History, Earlham College
Richmond, IN

"Beautifully designed, both editorially and visually, *Celebrating Whittier: America's 1907 Centennial* provides context for the bicentennial celebrations as well as the significant role of the Whittier Home Association in preserving and interpreting Whittier's legacy since 1898.

— *Tordis Ilg Isselhardt, Publisher and interpretive consultant*
Images from the Past
Bennington, VT

"This is a wonderful book about Mr. Whittier with many pictures and information about how people in 1907 regarded him and his contributions to our nation."

The Whittier Museum Gazette
Myra Hilliard, Director
Whittier Historical Society and Museum
Whittier, CA

Celebrating Whittier
New England's Quaker Poet and Abolitionist

*May this broaden
your knowledge of J G W
& his legacy —*

Pamela J Ferrenn

Celebrating Whittier
New England's Quaker Poet and Abolitionist
America's 1907 Centennial

Compiled and Edited by
Pamela Johnson Fenner

Michaelmas Press
Amesbury, Massachusetts

Celebrating Whittier
New England's Quaker Poet and Abolitionist
America's 1907 Centennial

Printed in the United States of America

09 08 07   10 9 8 7 6 5 4 3 2

ISBN 0-9647832-2-3

Publisher's Cataloging-in-Publication
(Provided by Quality Books, Inc.)

Fenner, Pamela J.
     Celebrating Whittier : New England's Quaker poet and
  abolitionist : America's 1907 centennial / compiled and
  edited by Pamela Johnson Fenner.
       p. cm.
     Includes bibliographical references and index.
     ISBN-13: 978-0-9647832-2-5
     ISBN-10: 0-9647832-2-3

     1. Whittier, John Greenleaf, 1807-1892. 2. Poets,
  American--19th century--Biography. 3. Abolitionists--
  United States--Biography.   I. Title.

  PS3285.F46 2008   811'.3
                           QBI08-600172

Design/layout: Pamela J. Fenner
Cover layout: Noelle Grattan, Image Wise
Copy editor: Kristine Hunt

In memory of
Elizabeth (Lizzie) Whittier Pickard
and Emily Binney Smith

CONTENTS

FOREWORD

Collected here are the numerous documents, photographs, and reproductions that record a proud nation's tribute to the Quaker, poet, journalist, and one of America's early abolitionists, John Greenleaf Whittier, at the 1907 Centennial celebration of his birth.

At that time, fifteen years after his death, Whittier remained one of the most popular poets in America. Indeed only Longfellow, whose Centennial was celebrated the same year, surpassed his fame and appeal. Hundreds of celebrations were held throughout the country from Boston to Chicago to California, with the special ceremonies and talks highlighted in the communities where Whittier lived — Haverhill and Amesbury, Massachusetts.

To commemorate the present day observance of Whittier's 200th Anniversary, Pamela Fenner, a past president of the Whittier Home Association, has reconstructed this 1907 celebration in amazing detail and scope. Not only has she compiled listings of the various Whittier observances and included photographs of attendees along with reproductions of programs, but she has also included the texts of the main presentations given at that time.

The addresses of Dr. Booker T. Washington in Amesbury, Professor Bliss Perry in Haverhill, William Lloyd Garrison, Jr. in Newburyport, Frank B. Sanborn in Salem, and Thomas W. Higginson in Boston are reprinted here and in aggregate reflect the high estimation that this age put upon Whittier's poems and his struggle to free the slaves. One of the many treasures found in the collection is a letter of tribute from President Theodore Roosevelt.

Among the various talks, exhibitions, and displays presented this year in celebration of the Whittier anniversary, this collection will surely remain a permanent contribution. Most significantly, it gives the reader an understanding of the central role that Whittier played in American letters and history during the nineteenth century and the reverence his own contemporaries had for his life and work.

—John "Ben" Pickard, Whittier scholar and co-author
Whittier and Whittierland: Portrait of a Poet and His World
Retired Professor of English, University of Florida
and great-grandnephew of John Greenleaf Whittier

PREFACE

John Greenleaf Whittier left a legacy far greater than his popular "SnowBound" bestseller of the 1860s. He was a New England farmer, committed Quaker, shoemaker, teacher, published poet, journalist, editor, politician, legislator, social reformer, abolition activist, library trustee, school board member, Harvard overseer, mentor to women writers—and devoted son, brother, uncle, nephew, neighbor, citizen, and friend of many.

When he died in 1892, the nation mourned. Newspaper accounts reported that thousands of people came to Amesbury to pay their respects at his home, attend the service, and visit the cemetery. Schools were closed the day of his funeral.

Fifteen years later—in 1907, the year of his Centennial birth—one could ask if people's regard for him and his contributions had changed in a brand new century given the expected shifts in cultural perspectives.

Just before the century ended, a committed group of women in Amesbury established the Whittier Home Association to preserve his home and memory. In fact, its first president initiated the town-wide Centennial planning. More than a century later, the organization continues to be the steward of his home, collections, and legacy. As a member of the exhibit committee of this association and preparing for the Bicentennial in 2007, I chose the Centennial of Whittier's birth for my research topic. This book is the culmination of this two-year project.

I enjoyed reading the treasure trove in the Whittier Home scrapbooks: letters, mementos, and clippings from century-old newspapers. There were articles from almost one hundred newspapers represented, but our local ones held a particular interest. The *Amesbury Daily News*, as with other newspapers in 1907, produced several editions per day. Within hours of the Centennial festivities, they were sharing the news with the citizenry. Many private groups and periodicals observed the anniversary over a year's time.

I discovered that the Whittier Centennial or "Centenary" of 1907 was an extraordinary event—one of the most important commemorations in the history of Amesbury, Haverhill, and Essex County. I also learned that it was recognized and celebrated in Boston, New York, Washington, Chicago, and other big cities and small towns all across America and even worldwide.

Whittier was truly a beloved man, and as the American population moved westward in the nineteenth century, people of all walks of life took the Whittier name with them, using it for the names of schools, libraries, parks, and even a town. Whittier, California was settled by Quakers and named for him during his lifetime.

The local 1907 Centennial observances were all-day events with programs of long and short speeches, readings of letters from noteworthy people who could not attend, instrumental and choral musical selections, and recitations of Whittier's poems as well as commemorative poems. Several leading abolitionists spoke at more than one Centennial commemoration.

Some orators were the social activists and reformers of their time. They lamented that while slavery had been abolished, the full freedoms that Whittier (and others) had sought so fervently had yet to be achieved. Their appeals to President Theodore Roosevelt remind one of the rhetoric of Martin Luther King, Jr. and others during the 1960s Civil Rights Movement.

The formal addresses are inspiring. Each reflects a particular framework of the orator. Frank Sanborn's address, for example, gives interesting details about Whittier's role as a skilled and resourceful politician in U.S. history. I have retained the original spelling and punctuation, but have broken the speeches into shorter paragraphs and added sub-headings for more clarity and ease of reading.

Another century has passed and once again his birth is being recognized and celebrated in Essex County and elsewhere. Though he has been less well-known due in part to the shifts in literary criticism, Whittier's poetry continues to be published and English and history scholars are offering fresh analyses of his literary and political contributions. New England school groups and tourists from around the world continue to visit his Haverhill and Amesbury homes.

Many teachers and parents view Whittier as an example of an authentic "hero" for our youth—a man whose poverty, lack of formal education, and countless obstacles did not prevent him from living according to his strong values. He risked his life and livelihood to work on behalf of a cause that was not just highly unpopular, but in fact, a dangerous one—the abolition of slavery. Even in this new century it continues to be fought in many countries.

Today as Americans prepare to participate in the 2008 Presidential primaries, caucuses, and election, we can feel proud that Whittier supported another unpopular cause—the women's suffrage movement.

—*Pamela Johnson Fenner, 2007*

Note: The publisher and the Whittier Home Association welcome any additional information or material on the Centennial celebrations.

AMESBURY

Plans for a town-wide Centennial celebration of the birth of John Greenleaf Whittier began in mid-1907. Since it had been only fifteen years since his death, there were many friends, neighbors, and colleagues—both near and far—who were still alive and remembered him with admiration, respect, and reverence.

Whittier had moved to Amesbury, Massachusetts in 1836 at age twenty-nine and resided there until his death in 1892. The family had sold his birthplace, the rural family farm in East Haverhill, and his brother, Matthew Franklin, planned to marry and move to Maine. John and his widowed mother, Abigail Hussey Whittier, purchased a four-room cottage with an attic on a small parcel of land near the center of Amesbury, not far from the mills. Also living with them were his unmarried maternal aunt, Mercy Hussey, and his sister, Elizabeth.

It was a fortuitous move for the family. The Whittiers were Quakers and choosing Amesbury meant they would be nearer to the Friends Meeting House, which they attended regularly. Amesbury was less isolated than his boyhood home, had a train station, which Whittier used for his travels, and was perhaps more welcoming to social reformers than other communities. The area's fields, hills, lakes, the Powow and Merrimac Rivers, as well as the beaches along the Atlantic provided much natural beauty and inspired many of Whittier's poems.

Although he traveled, visited friends and relatives, and took extensive vacations, 86 Friend Street was where he called "home." It was there he penned much of his literary legacy, including his most famous work, "Snow-Bound." Unlike the homes of his writing colleagues, Hawthorne, Emerson, and Longfellow, who had large, grand houses, Whittier's remained simple even after adding more rooms over the years. He also supervised the construction of the present Quaker Meeting House in 1850.

Whittier at age twenty-nine

Until the Civil War, he led a crusade against slavery, serving at the local, state, and national levels. These abolitionist activities also brought risks to his personal safety as well as his literary reputation.

In 1866, after the war, he published "Snow-Bound," which was based on his childhood memories. With its success, Whittier no longer had to struggle financially and was able to lead a comfortable life supported by his writing. He was a major contributor to *The Atlantic Monthly*, founded in 1857, and enjoyed a wide public following. His great-grand-nephew, John "Ben" Pickard, wrote about Whittier's life:

> In his years in Amesbury, Whittier was secure and content, enjoying a close association with his neighbors. He could often be found talking shop with Amesbury residents at a local store and spent many hours in the back room of John Hume's tailor shop talking about literature and politics. A biographer once commented that his poetry was written first of all for the neighbors and that remains the central truth about his writing: his best poetry had strong local roots.
>
> As an Amesbury resident, he wrote poems for local events, served on the school committee, purchased books for the library, attended temperance rallies, secured speakers for the local lecture series, and, while on the School Board, defended the need of social recreation for young people.

On his seventieth birthday Whittier wrote to his Amesbury neighbors:

> Forty years ago I came to dwell among you…[and] your interests and welfare are mine; there is not a face among you that I shall not always be glad to see; not a rod of soil on the Merrimac or Powow that I shall not be happy to retread; and about my hearth-fire in the old house on Friend Street I shall hope often to meet you.

Artist's rendition of how the original house might have looked[1]

*Last known photograph of Whittier (left) in Hampton Falls, NH
in 1892 taken by his nephew, Greenleaf Whittier, age fifteen*

3

Although Whittier had hoped he would die in his home as did his mother and sister, he suffered a stroke during a vacation in Hampton Falls, New Hampshire and died a few days later. Ben Pickard described the following days:

> His funeral on September 10, 1892, of course, took place from the Amesbury house. The house was draped in black, his body was displayed in the parlor and an estimated 5000 people trooped through to view the body. The funeral service took place in the garden behind the house with over a 1000 people jammed in the area, in trees, on fences, and crowded in the surrounding streets. He was then buried in the Quaker section of Union Cemetery in a family plot that contained all the members of his family.

Lizzie Whittier Pickard

Whittier's home then became the property of his married niece, Elizabeth Whittier Pickard. Named for Whittier's sister, but always called "Lizzie," she lived in Portland, Maine with her husband, Samuel T. Pickard, and son, Greenleaf.

She had moved to Whittier's home in Amesbury in 1858 at age thirteen, attending school and later caring for her ill namesake. After Elizabeth's death, she ran the household and by 1864 acted as hostess and travelled with her uncle. Ben Pickard noted that as Whittier's most intimate confidante, she functioned as a "surrogate daughter, devoted sister and loving helpmate in one." Following her marriage to S. T. in 1876, Whittier moved between Amesbury, Danvers, and elsewhere, living with relatives and friends.

Honoring the Poet

Following his death, there was increasing community interest in honoring Whittier. Locally, these efforts were led by Emily Binney Smith, a close friend of Lizzie. She founded and was elected the first president of the Whittier Home Association on January 26, 1898, following a split from the Elizabeth Whittier Club, which she had also helped found two years earlier. Smith would go on to serve as president for twenty-eight continuous years. This new association was encouraged in its efforts to preserve the poet's home by Lizzie, who served as a vice-president.

Lizzie leased the Home to the association for $5 per year and helped refurbish the house. She returned the furniture and other items she possessed or

Emily B. Smith, President of Whittier Home Association

could find so that the house was made to look as much as possible as when the poet lived there. Mrs. Smith, a widow with a young daughter, Gertrude, accepted the members' invitation to live in the residence rent-free as curator.

The Home was open to active members every day except Sundays and each could have a key to the Home. Members could be admitted by their own key any time from 9 am to 5 pm, but after hours, they were required to ring the bell. The general public was admitted three days per week—Tuesdays, Thursdays, and Saturdays—for a fee of 10 cents from 9 am to 5 pm. The fee for children was 5 cents. Association records note that the visitors' collection box contained $20.70 at the end of the year.[2]

The Whittier Home Association became quite popular and its active membership roster of seventy-five women was kept filled. Their register shows that an increasingly large number of visitors came to the Home, many from long distances. The members always observed the poet's birthday, continuing a decades-long tradition of Whittier's friends and admirers.

When Lizzie died in 1902, her husband, S. T., decided to move into the Home with son Greenleaf and his wife. S. T. was also Whittier's first biographer and wanted to finish his life in the Home where he could preserve and operate the main part of the house as a museum for visitors, while adding a new ell to accommodate his family.

However, proposed changes in occupancy created some tensions among the family, the association, and residents as to how the home/museum would be managed.[3] In time, these changes were accepted and Mrs. Smith and the association moved across the street to 4 Pleasant (now Pickard) Street ,continuing its mission as written in the 1903 Articles of Incorporation to "celebrate suitably the poet's birthday, and promote any movements for philanthropy, education, or reform which such a memorial society may properly assist."

S. T. Pickard

Amesbury home of John Greenleaf Whittier
1st site of Whittier Home Association
86 Friend Street 1907

2nd site of Whittier Home Association
Pleasant Street, now Pickard Street
across the street from Whittier's home

3rd site of Whittier Home Association
just before the 1907 Centennial
on Pickard Street

Home of John Greenleaf Whittier and
present site of Whittier Home Association
2007 JGW Bicentennial

THE WHITTIER HOME ASSOCIATION
Original Membership List—February 9, 1898

*The active membership of the Whittier Home Association was limited
to seventy-five and was filled shortly after the association was organized.
The following made up the first full quota:*

Mesdames:

A. H. Atwood
H. L. Bailey
S. R. Bailey
W. E. Biddle
E. R. Briggs
R. E. Briggs
M. A. Brown
G. Cammett
G. W. Cate
E. A. Childs
J. T. Choate
Seth Clark
C. F. Clement
L. Currier
S. A. Dennett
A. Dennett
C. Ellis
H. M. Estes
A. H. Fielden
A. Frankle
G. W. George
A. N. Gove
W. W. Hawkes
S. Hill

A. M. Horton
J. H. Howarth
F. M. Hoyt
James Hume
John Hume
I. H. Little
C. W. Long
M. D. Mason
D. W. Maxfield
F. S. Merrill
F. W. Merrill
C. A. Nayson
C. E. Osgood
E. Osgood
G. W. Osgood
A. N. Parry
B. W. Pettingell
S. T. Pickard
S. Purrington
C. F. Robinson
E. H. Rowell
A. B. Russell
J. Sargent
E. B. Smith
M. D. F. Steer
M. A. True

M. Turner
A. C. Webster
F. N. Wheelock
B. H. Young

Misses:

J. Biddle
H. Biddle
M. E. Carter
A. Childs
E. Childs
G. Clark
Susan Clark
D. Dolbier
G. Fielden
A. Follansbee
Elizabeth Hume
A. Huntington
L. C. Osgood
J. Sargent
T. H. Soper
J. Sparhawk
F. Sparhawk
E. Woolfenden
E. C. Woolfenden

The formal organization was effected February 9, 1898 with the first three officers:

President, Mrs. E. B. Smith
Secretary, Mrs. E. H. Rowell
Treasurer, Miss Emma C. Woolfenden

Centennial Planning

Emily Binney Smith initiated the planning for a town-wide celebration of Whittier's birth, calling a meeting of Amesbury's leaders in June of 1907. Out of that gathering came a committee chaired by the Honorable George W. Cate, Judge of the Second District Court, and with whom the poet resided at the Home the last years of his life. Mrs. Smith was secretary, and other members of the committee were: Mrs. John H. Howarth, James H. Hassett, Selectman Cyrus W. Rowell, Samuel T. Pickard, and Rev. James D. Dingwell. Various subcommittees were also formed to handle the arrangements for the reception, hospitality, music, and decorations. [See Appendix]

An energetic woman, Smith had already started a movement in 1901 to collect funds for a permanent statue to be located in some public place in Amesbury. The women of the Whittier Home solicited money by writing more than 5,000 letters to women's clubs and individuals, not just locally, but worldwide. By November 1906, the association had collected more than $5,000 in money and pledges for this purpose. The celebration in 1907 proved to be a catalyst to generate additional funds. In 1918 they purchased the original house with the funds—a decision Whittier might well have thought more appropriate than erecting a statue.

The Whittier Statue.

The Whittier Home Association was the first to propose a statue to the memory of the poet Whittier, and when it shall have been completed it will also stand as a monument to the untiring devotion of the ladies who are included in that organization.

At the mid-summer meeting of the association, July 4, 1901, held in the garden of the Whittier home on Friend street, the president, Mrs. Emily B. Smith, made the announcement that it was proposed to erect a statue to Whittier in Amesbury, and the sum named was $500, towards which the association then pledged $300.

This gift was followed by Mrs. S. T. Pickard, she pledging $500. It was soon found that the first-named sum would be insufficient for a memorial in keeping with the reputation of the man it was to commemorate and the desired amount was advanced to $10,000. _1

George W. Cate, Chair

8

Mrs. Emily B. Smith,
President.

Miss Emma C. Woolfenden,
Treasurer

Mrs. Edward H. Rowell
Cor. Secretary

WHITTIER HOME ASSOCIATION
OF AMESBURY.

STATUE · FUND

"And thou, O Land he loved, rejoice
That in the countless years to come,
Whenever Freedom needs a voice,
These sculptured lips shall not be dumb!"
("One of the Signers"---Whittier)

It is proposed to erect a statue of John Greenleaf Whittier in Amesbury, Massachusetts, his home for over fifty years, in which the greater part of his life work was done.

It is planned to do this by voluntary contributions from those to whom Mr. Whittier's memory is dear either as a reformer or as a poet.

The memorial will be from a design made by some sculptor of established and wide reputation, and will cost not less than ten thousand dollars.

The designs submitted will be examined and decided upon by the Statue Committee of the Whittier Home Association of Amesbury, and an Advisory Board whose names are here given.

Contributions may be sent to Miss Emma C. Woolfenden of Amesbury, Massachusetts, treasurer of the Whittier Home Association; whether large or small they will be gratefully received and immediately acknowledged.

ADVISORY BOARD.

Mr. Edmund Clarence Stedman, Bronxville, N. Y.
Hon. John Hay, Washington, D. C.
Hon. Geo. F. Hoar, Worcester, Mass.
Mr. S. T. Pickard, Boston, Mass.
Rev. Lyman Abbott D. D., New York.
Hon. Geo. von L. Meyer, Hamilton, Mass.
Rev. Theodore L. Cuyler D. D. Brooklyn, N. Y
Mr. Joshua L. Baily, Philadelphia, Pa.
Mr. Bliss Perry, Boston, Mass.
Dr. Booker T. Washington, Tuskegee, Ala.
Hon. Murat Halstead, Cincinnati, O.
Pres. Wm. F. Slocum, Colorado College, Col.
Capt. Charles L. Mitchell, Boston, Mass.
Mr. Charles L. Hutchinson, Chicago, Ill.
Mr. Francis J. Garrison, Boston, Mass.
Hon. Milton M. Fisher, Medway, Mass.
Hon. Robert T. Davis, Fall River, Mass.
Mr. Charles H. Davis, Mystic, Conn.
Mr. Wm. L. Darling, St. Paul, Minn.
Hon. Alden P. White, Salem, Mass.
Mr. James Hume, Amesbury, Mass.
Mr. Seth Clark, Amesbury, Mass.
Hon. Geo. W. Cate, Amesbury, Mass.
Mr. S. R. Bailey, Amesbury, Mass.

Whittier Home Association formed 1898
Occupied Whittier Home first of June 1902
Merrill House 1903 to 1907
Colby House 1907.
Centennial Dec 1907.

Waiting for the Amesbury Train are Dean Howe,
Dr. Samuel E. Courtney, and Dr. Robert E. Park

Postcard from the Salisbury Point Railroad Historical Society showing the local station around
1884 in its old position — before it was moved close to the town — the other side of the Back River.

"Amesbury Does Itself Proud,"
read one headline in a local newspaper.
December 17, 1907 arrived and the festivities were blessed with beneficent weather.
Newspaper accounts of that day heralded
the arrival of a late morning train bringing
the distinguished speakers and guests from
Boston. The president of the Boston and
Maine Railroad, Lucius Tuttle, made the
arrangements. Since there were more than
two-hundred traveling from Boston, extra
cars had to be added to the train.

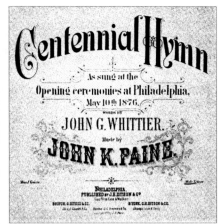

When the group from Boston grew to an
unexpectedly large size, the Amesbury greet-
ers had to adjust their plans. The luncheon was the most ambitious event the association had organized since their founding less than a decade earlier. The arriving
guests were divided into two groups.

The first was taken by carriages to the new home of the Whittier Home
Association on Pleasant Street (now Pickard Street). The second group went
to the Friends' Meetinghouse and the Whittier Home until they could walk to
the associations' headquarters for the luncheon. Undaunted, the Hospitality
Committee managed to feed the dignitaries in two sittings.

Amesbury's Town Hall auditorium and balcony were filled to capacity and
citizens were turned away due to the limited space. The *Amesbury Daily News* reported in the evening edition:

> …laurel ropes were extended over the proscenium arch. Large American flags
> and the State shield were at the rear of the stage on front of the balcony, while
> on stage front was the fine picture of Mr. Whittier, the property of the High
> School, which was painted by Charles E. Davis, the celebrated artist who is a
> native of this town.[4]

More than sixty guests and Amesbury's Centennial Committee filled the stage. The
Amesbury Daily News announced that "It was a brilliant audience such as the town
has seldom seen before." Orchestral selections accompanied the guests as they arrived in the hall. A chorus of one-hundred school children sang two of Whittier's
poems set to music, including "The Centennial Hymn."[5] The Market Street Baptist quartet and Mrs. Sadie Gale Taylor sang other selections. After the speeches
and presentations, the Centennial ceremonies closed with everyone singing
"America." The extraordinary day closed with guests returning to the Whittier
Home Association for tea.

==

Order of Exercises

❦

Concert Programme
By
Whitman Fest Orchestra

Overture, "Poet and Peasant"	.	Suppe
Selection, "Faust"	.	Gounod
Violin Solos, { "Serenata"	.	Moszkowski
"Serenade Badine"	.	Marie
"Hezre Kati"	.	Hubay
Fantasie, "Dying Poet"	.	Gottschalk
Selection, "Rienzi"	.	Wagner

Singing, "Centennial Hymn" . . . .

Chorus of School Children

Invocation . . . .

Rev. A. E. Dunning, D.D.

Introductory Greeting . . . . . .

Hon. George W. Cate

Reading of Letter from President Roosevelt . . .

Hon. Alden P. White

Greeting of the Commonwealth . . . . .

Hon. William M. Olin, *Secretary of the Commonwealth*

Singing, "Dream of Summer" . . . . . .

Quartette

Order of Exercises

A Word of Welcome to Whittier's Friends, from Mrs. Annie Fields
Hon. Alden P. White

Address . . . .
Hon. John D. Long

Address . . . .
Hon. John L. Bates

Solo, "The Eternal Goodness" . . . . . .
Mrs. Sadie Gale Taylor

Address . . . .
Dr. Booker T. Washington

Singing, "Hurrah! the Seaward Breezes" . . . .
Quartette

Reading of Letters from Edmund Clarence Stedman and Dr. Amory H. Bradford
Hon. Alden P. White

Address . . . .
Edwin D. Mead

Address . . . .
Hon. David Cross

Singing, "A Christmas Carmen" . . . . . .
Chorus of School Children

Singing, "America" . . . .
School Children, Orchestra and Audience

Dr. Booker T. Washington

Washington Hails Whittier

The Centennial Committee could not have selected a more appropriate guest speaker for its tribute to Whittier than Dr. Booker T. Washington (1856-1915)—educator, author, orator, and the foremost African-American at the turn of the century.

Born of a black slave woman and a nearby white farmer on a farm in Virginia, he struggled to obtain an education after Emancipation. Washington was an alumnus of the Hampton Institute and, at the time of the Centennial, the first president of Tuskegee University in Alabama.

His book, *Up From Slavery: An Autobiography*, had been published in 1900. On a previous visit to Amesbury, he gave a speech at the Whittier Home Association on July 4, 1901.

WASHINGTON'S ADDRESS

In common with the citizens of our entire country, I am sure that my race joins in most hearty thanks to the people of Amesbury for keeping alive in so fitting a manner the memory of the poet, John Greenleaf Whittier. The celebration in which we are engaged today in this town is but additional evidence of cause for gratitude to you.

The one hundredth anniversary of the birth of John Greenleaf Whittier marks a fitting occasion upon which to review the progress of a race in which he was so deeply and helpfully interested. The life of such a man marks a milestone in the life of a race and a nation. You who are gathered here, as well as the entire nation, will agree with me in stating that the influence of John Greenleaf Whittier in America was never more potent than today, that he lives in the hearts, in the ambitions and in the activities

of thousands of men and women throughout the country.

In the larger and deeper sense no one would say that Ralph Waldo Emerson, William Lloyd Garrison, Phillips Brooks, and a host of other similar characters are dead. With each recurring anniversary of such great souls, they knit their lives and their deeds more deeply and more closely into the hearts and actions of all of our countrymen.

In an especial degree, however, are the people of the race with which I am proud to be identified, grateful that such a man as John Greenleaf Whittier lived. In an especial degree do we have cause to cherish his memory and to participate in this anniversary occasion?

As I speak to you today, representing in some measure the feeling of the ten millions of black people in America, I recall

14

the courage and the degree of self-effacement that were required in the case of Whittier in placing himself, at the time he did, upon the side of the weak, the oppressed, the enslaved. He might have turned his great talents in another direction and received larger temporary reward and a wider degree of temporary fame, but he chose the "better part," and in so choosing he made a contribution to the freedom of a race and to the perpetuity of a country that will live through the ages.

When fire comes into contact with dynamite or powder, something happens. The two cannot dwell together in peace; so, when the experiment was tried of having such a soul as that of John Greenleaf Whittier inhabit the same country with slavery, the outcome was failure. Slavery with its results could not live in peace in the same atmosphere with Whittier. When slavery touched this great soul, something happened. So the history of the civilized world teaches that human bondage and oppression cannot dwell in peace where there is one courageous, brave spirit constantly striving toward the right.

The name of John Greenleaf Whittier is a household word in the homes of the black people of this country. While this celebration is taking place on the spot, which he loved so much here in Massachusetts, there is another celebration that is in progress throughout the South among the people of my race. I recall, as an example that there is located upon the grounds of the Hampton Institute in Virginia, a little school for the primary children known as "The Whittier School." There his name and memory are kept green. There today hundreds of little voices are joining in songs of praise and gratitude. It is in such schools and in the hearts of such children that Whittier will most live in the future.

Portrait of Whittier by
Charles E. Davis

The custom is to express gratitude to such men as Garrison and Whittier for bringing about the liberation of the black man in America, but theirs was a larger and more lasting work. Their efforts resulted in the liberation of two races, the white and black. More than this, their efforts resulted in the liberation of two sections of our country.

As a result of their work, the black man is in a larger measure free today to help the white man. The white man is free to help the Negro. The North is free to assist the South. The South is free to partake in all that concerns the North. It is this larger and broader freedom that has resulted in the most good to our country.

But what of the result of Whittier's work and Whittier's faith? Was he right? Was his faith misplaced? Most that he hoped for and worked for has already taken place. We have a potent example in the case of the more than ten million Negroes who, in the face of difficulties, have accumulated

PRESIDENT ROOSEVELT'S
TRIBUTE TO WHITTIER

THE WHITE HOUSE
WASHINGTON

Oyster Bay, N. Y.,
July 9, 1907.

My Dear Mrs. Smith:

It is with very real regret that I find myself unable to accept your invitation to be present at Amesbury on the occasion of the one hundredth anniversary of the birth of Whittier. I have always felt a peculiar affection and reverence for the "good Quaker poet." I do not for one moment subscribe to the belief that we can divorce the art of the artist, and especially the art of the man of letters, from character, and from the teachings that mould character. It seems to me that all good Americans should feel a peculiar pride in Whittier, exactly because he combined the power of expression, and the great gift of poetry, with a flaming zeal for righteousness which made him a leader in matters of the spirit no less than of the intellect.

Faithfully yours,
THEODORE ROOSEVELT.

MRS. EMILY B. SMITH,
 4 Pleasant Street,
  Amesbury, Massachusetts.

BOOKER T WASHINGTON HON. JOHN D. LONG
THE PRINCIPAL SPEAKERS AT THE CELEBRATION

The 100th Anniversary of the Poet's Birth.

Distinguished Persons at Exercises in Amesbury.

His Work for Humanity the Keynote of Speeches.

AMESBURY, Dec 17—As simple and as unostentatious as the life and character of the great poet himself was the centenary celebration of the birth of John G. Whittier by the town, which was his home for more than half a century. Not a flag was to be seen in the streets. Not a house was decorated in honor of his memory. There was no parade. An informal reception at the headquarters of the Whittier home association and literary exercises at the town hall comprised the whole of the celebration.

And yet the very quietness of the event harmonized well with the gentle nature of the poet. The celebration, arranged by old friends and neighbors and by those who knew him well, could not have been displeasing to his modest taste, and there was not a word of extravagant eulogy in the numerous addresses or in the letters that were read at the literary exercises. Amesbury has good reason to felicitate itself upon the success of the celebration, which was carried out by the Whittier home association, assisted by a citizens' committee.

Whittier was a poet, but it was not those who celebrated the anniversary of his birth, in fact. Hon John D. Long was the only poet among the speakers, and it has been many years since he published his translation of Virgil's Aeneid There was one other poet on the platform—Sam Walter Foss of Somerville—and in the audience were George Birdseye of Lynn and Miss Sarah Orne Jewett of Boston, but if there were other poets present they are unknown to fame.

Conspicuous Figures.

The conspicuous figures in the celebration were public men, judges, clergymen and Whittier's personal friends. Not what the poet did for literature, but what he accomplished for humanity, was the burden of the addresses and the letters. Booker T. Washington spoke with his characteristic eloquence of Whittier's services in the antislavery cause. Edwin D. Mead struck a different vein. He dwelt upon Whittier's great interest in the movement for peace and universal disarmament, deprecating the martial tendency of the present administration and the love of war which seems manifest in the spirit of the nation.

There was only moderate applause, in which, however, most of those on the platform joined, when Mr Mead said:

"Whittier was not only the poet of antislavery, but he also took part with the other New England poets in the crusade against war. One of the things which would have saddened Whittier today is the fact that our own republic is hastening to take upon herself the methods of the hoary old nations of Europe.

"We see in the newspapers the interest of the American people in the great armada sweeping from one sea to another. You cannot conceive Whittier greeting with a pean an American pageant like that. You cannot conceive of an ode from Emerson or Longfellow on America's appearance as the sender of a great armada, as the newspapers call it.

"Whittier would have been saddened at that, and would have been saddened to hear the loud and urgent note of the American administration today for

Local newspaper clipping

more than \$350,000,000 worth of taxable property; who have acquired nearly half a million homes and farms; who have moved forward to the extent that 56 per cent can read and write the English languages; who have 16,000 Christian ministers and 24,000 church organizations, with \$27,000,000 worth of church property.

In 1833, Prudence Crandall was forbidden to open a little school in the state of Connecticut for the education of black children. Today there is scarcely a village or county in any section of America where the Negro child cannot be taught.

I do not speak as a pessimist. The world is going forward, not backward…. Whittier's work was not in vain.…No one is in a better position to realize this than I who belong to what is known as one of the unpopular or disadvantaged races.

In the solution of all of our problems, however, we are far from perfection; wrong and injustice still exist, and much serious work remains before the right shall completely triumph. For one, however, I like a hard, serious and perplexing problem at which to work. For myself I would not care to live in an age where there was no hard problem to solve or no portion of the human family to be helped or lifted up. To do it we must have more of the patience, of the courage of the spirit of Whittier. In our haste and shortness of vision

We are often too prone to depend upon the passing of mere statutory laws to settle serious problems. The most fundamental and vital things of life are above and beyond the control of statutory laws.…

True, all that Whittier and others prophesied has not come to pass in the manner that they wished for and hoped for, but this need not discourage or perplex us.…[Living up] to the perfect requirement of the Golden Rule and the Ten Commandments…are goals toward which humanity is constantly striving.

Let us all, as we tread upon this sacred soil today, feel more grateful for the life and deeds of the man whose anniversary we celebrate, and let us here all rededicate ourselves to the uncompleted task which he left with us, **in** his words always remembering that:

The changeless laws of Justice bind
Oppressor with oppressed;
And close as sin and suffering joined,
We march to fate abreast.

To feel the emotion, the sheer excitement of the day and its historical import for local residents, one essay stands out, published December 18, 1907 in the *New Leader*, a local newspaper.

THE CENTENNIAL EXERCISES
By Frank M. Prescott

Whittier the poet, Whittier the man, was extolled in this his home town yesterday in a manner that shows the best asset of Amesbury to be the name of John Greenleaf Whittier, the Quaker poet, who for more than half a century walked the streets of this home town by adoption.

No more distinguished assembly had gathered to do honor to an honored son than that which yesterday filled the Town Hall to its doors, and had an auditorium been available twice its size, it would have been inadequate to do obeisance at the shrine of Whittier.

The celebration was in every way of the town, which was his home for 56 years. It was here that he did his life-work; it was here that he walked his streets and went in and out before the citizens, a benediction to all who were acquainted with him; it was here that men of note turned in the hour of their country's need; it was to this hamlet the eyes of the nation were directed during the reconstruction period, and it was eminently fitting that yesterday the thought of the world should be centered on this town, the home of the poet of emancipation.

The day was all that could be desired and when the sun arose in all its splendor, the hearts of Amesbury's citizens were filled with gratitude that the elements were to fittingly aid them in celebrating the birth of an honored son.

Many visitors arrived during the early forenoon and spent the time in visiting many places of interest made historic by their associations with Whittier's poems, but the large number were introduced to "Whittierland," at the noon hour, upon the arrival of the train from Boston.

President Lucius Tuttle of the Boston & Maine railroad actively co-operated, and kindly sent a car direct to Amesbury from Boston. Some had made the prediction that it would not be needed, but when it was found that in place of one car, two were crowded and that more than 200 citizens of the Commonwealth had journeyed to Amesbury to participate in the exercises, the success of the celebration was assured.

Mr. W. W. Hawkes, chairman of the reception committee, accompanied by Representative Samuel L. Porter and Charles I. Pettingell, met the train at Newburyport and welcomed the guests in behalf of the citizens of Amesbury. The work of the reception committee was done in a thorough manner, and...the party was divided, and one-half of the delegation [was] in charge of A. N. Pary while the the remainder of the guests [were] in charge of James H. Hassett.

[Guests] were received by the poet's biographer, Mr. Samuel T. Pickard. The Friends meeting house, too, was not neglected. It was nearly time for the exercises to commence at the Town Hall when the last guest had partaken of the dainty lunch prepared by the ladies of the association....

The exercises at the Town Hall were of a high order and it is doubtful if as large a number of notable people were ever before gathered in Amesbury, except at the funeral of the beloved poet, as filled the place of meeting yesterday.

It was in every respect a cosmopolitan gathering, as the man of letters and the humble day laborer sat side by side and drank in the inspiration that was drawn from the noble life, which the exercises of the day commemorated. Men who have stood high in the councils of the state, members of the judiciary, disciples of Blackstone, men of business, and authors of note; in fact, the representation of every walk in life, bowed in humble reverence while the Divine blessing was invoked by the Rev. Dunning D.D. of Boston.

While there was disappointment that some who had been expected to grace the occasion were unable to be present, it was the consensus of all who participated "that Amesbury had paid a fitting tribute to the memory of the much beloved citizen and shown that a prophet, in the person of Whittier, had been honored in his own country."

While the secretary of state, William M. Olin, was unable to be present, the greetings of the Commonwealth were gracefully spoken by Judge Edgar J. Sherman....The address of ex-Governor John D. Long was a scholarly tribute to the worth of the man as a poet and citizen.

When Dr. Booker T. Washington rose to voice the gratitude of a race that Whittier aided in emancipating, he was given a royal reception and it was several minutes before he could proceed with his address.

The Dr.'s address was polished, enlightening, and held the attention of his hearers, while he sketched what the colored race had accomplished in less than half a century, and his tribute to Whittier was most fitting.

The address of Edwin D. Mead dealt with Whittier as a poet, and his analysis showed him not a whit behind the other poets of his time, who had traveled more extensively than had Whittier, and thus aided their imagination by the use of what their eyes had seen.

Did one wish for New England scenes, the speaker pointed him to "Snow-Bound" and "School Days." Thus the audience was led to see, by various allusions, that the poet's was a well-rounded intellect.

The selection of the Honorable Alden P. White of Salem to read the letters was a most happy thought on the part of the committee and he performed the work assigned him in an excellent manner. [He] stated that the number of women's clubs that had contributed [to the Statue Fund] was 113, giving $401.

At the conclusion of the exercises at the Town Hall, the Whittier Home Association kept open house and served tea.

Newspaper clipping showing members of the Whittier Home Association hosting luncheon for special guests.

19

HAVERHILL

In 1907, Haverhill citizens, proud of their native son, were also making plans for a Centennial celebration. The family farm where John Greenleaf Whittier was born on December 17, 1807 was located in East Haverhill, on which a two-and-a half-story house had been built by his great-great-grandfather, Thomas Whittier, around 1688.

He was the first son and second child of John and Abigail (Hussey) Whittier. Known within the family as Greenleaf, he grew up with his parents, a brother, and two sisters along with his Aunt Mercy and Uncle Moses. This rather isolated, rural setting provided the children with hills, meadows, pastures, a running brook, and woodlands in which to play.

With the poor farm land, everyone had to work hard to maintain the homestead. Whittier was not physically suited to farm work, but enjoyed most of the outdoor life growing up. He and his siblings took turns going to the Friends Meetings, as the chaise was too small for all the children to fit in.

They had few books, but the Bible was regularly read aloud and there was storytelling. Very little formal education was possible, so he was grateful to those who let him borrow books, especially his first teacher, Joshua Coffin, who lent him Robert Burns' poetry. Inspired, he began to write his own verses.

Whittier Homestead in Haverhill

When he was nineteen, Mary sent his poem, "The Exile's Departure" (unbeknownst to him), to the *Newburyport Free Press*, where the abolitionist William Lloyd Garrison was editor. She signed it "W. Haverhill, June 1, 1826." One poem after another was published and eventually, Garrison traveled to Haverhill to meet the young poet. He encouraged the family to find the means for Greenleaf to have more schooling. Through shoemaking and teaching, Whittier was able to afford to attend two terms at Haverhill Academy.

Interested in neither farming nor teaching, Whittier obtained editing jobs through Garrison's help at the *National Philanthropist, American Manufacturer,* and the *Essex Gazette*. For a year and half he lived in Hartford, Connecticut, where he edited the widely-read *New England Weekly Review.*

In 1831, he brought out a book of prose works, *Legends of New England,* and the next year returned to the Haverhill farm after his father's death. 1833 was a pivotal year, and with his published essay, "Justice and Expediency," Whittier became more involved with politics and vigorously committed himself to the antislavery movement.

Even though he had sold the Homestead and moved to Amesbury in 1836, memories of his Haverhill childhood would provide him with the subject matter and the sensitivity to write some of his best poems: "Snow-Bound," "In School-Days," "My Playmate," "Telling the Bees," and "The Barefoot Boy." He also wrote poems for several Haverhill events and commemorations.

Centennial Ticket

When Whittier was almost eighty years old, a group of admirers from Haverhill and Bradford established the Haverhill Whittier Club. The initial meeting was held at the home of James R. Nichols on February 16, 1886. Most, if not all, of the original members of the club knew Whittier personally in varying degrees. These friends and admirers came together to promote the further study of his writings and to collect unpublished poems or facts about his life. Every year they celebrated his birthday, and it would be a particularly festive event if Whittier were present to receive visitors.

Whittier's birthplace, often referred to as "The Homestead," was formally opened in 1893 after Haverhill's former mayor, James H. Carleton, purchased the property and presented it to the Haverhill Whittier Club. Since then, the Club's Board of Trustees has maintained the historic house and grounds for visitors in tribute to Whittier.

During the 1907 Centennial celebration, local newspapers reported that the Homestead was a "mecca for the sightseers," schools were closed, and hundreds of people came to attend the events. The City of Haverhill and the Whittier Club jointly held the main commemoration at the First Universalist Church, during which letters were read from literary persons around the country who were unable to attend.

Mrs. Julia Ward Howe of Boston,[6] best known for writing "The Battle Hymn of the Republic" during the Civil War, wrote a poem for the occasion. Bliss Perry (1860–1954), *The Atlantic Monthly* (1899–1909) gave the prime address. Perry had taught at Williams College, Princeton University, and was to later teach in Paris. He wrote extensively about Thomas Carlyle, Emerson, Whitman, and Whittier.

Franklin B. Sanborn, an early abolitionist from Concord,[7] offered personal reflections in a tribute. Prior to the program, guests were served a special luncheon at the Whittier Homestead with some of the food cooked on the open hearth.

The Citizens of Haverhill

request the honour of your presence

at the Commemoration of the one hundredth Birthday of

John Greenleaf Whittier

at the Universalist Church, Kenoza Avenue

on Tuesday afternoon, December the seventeenth

one thousand nine hundred and seven

at half after two o'clock

Addresses by

Mr. Frank B. Sanborn

Professor Bliss Perry

Poem by

Mrs. Julia Ward Howe

Roswell L. Wood

Mayor of Haverhill

Maurice D. Clarke, M. D.

President of Whittier Club

24

Order of Exercises

PRELUDE—Largo and Pastorale   *Guilmant*
    MR. JAMES W. HILL

PRAYER
    REV. SAMUEL C. BEANE

INTRODUCTION
    MAYOR R. L. WOOD

REMARKS
    REV. LEVI M. POWERS, D. D.

SINGING—Selected
    WEBER QUARTETTE

READING OF LETTERS
    MR. ALBERT L. BARTLETT

POEM
    MRS. JULIA WARD HOWE

Order of Exercises

SINGING—Whittier's " Christmas Song "
    WEBER QUARTETTE

PERSONAL REMINISCENCES
  OF WHITTIER
    MR. FRANK SANBORN

SINGING—Whittier's " Eternal Goodness"
    WEBER QUARTETTE

ADDRESS—The Formative Influences
  Which Affected Whittier's Career
    PROF. BLISS PERRY

HYMN—Whittier's " Our Master "
    AUDIENCE

POSTLUDE—Orgel Hymn   *Piutti*
    MR. JAMES W. HILL

Julia Ward Howe

WHITTIER

A spirit in our midst abode,
A champion, risking life and limb,
With firm intent to bear the load
That Fate had meted out to him:

The burthen of an evil time
That grieved men's souls with forfeit
   pledge;
The task, t'assail a Nation's crime
With weapon of celestial edge.

For still a son of Peace was he,
Servant and master of the lyre;
All bloodless must his warfare be,
Launched all in love, his bolts of fire.

Such victories are given to song
As slaughter never may achieve,
When the rapt soul is wooed from
   wrong
Some heavenly lessons to receive.

I saw him when his locks that crown
Fair youth were heaped above his brow;
His eyes like lustrous jewels shone
The trifler's world they did not know.

Feathered as from an angel's wing
The arrows of his quiver flew,
A thrill of sorrow they might bring,
A wound, and yet a balsam too.

Soon War's wild music filled the land,
And fields of fight were won and lost,
When grieving Conscience made her
   stand
To pay the debt of deadly cost.

And many were the days of dole
Before the bitter strife could cease.
But ever that anointed soul
Dwelt in its citadel of Peace.

Thence, like an anthem rising clear
Rang out the poet's helpful word,
Melodious messages of cheer
Above the battle din were heard.

And years of labor came and went,
But ere he passed the bound of Fate
His days were crowned with high
   content;
He saw his land regenerate.

. . . . .

   Methought that from the Poet's grave
A whisper thrilled the ear, that said:
Surrender not his music brave,
For while it live he is not dead.

And when, with other sounds of Earth
Shall pass the beauty of his rhyme,
Eternity shall keep the worth
Lost from the treasury of Time.

Bliss Perry

BLISS PERRY'S ADDRESS

The Formative Influences Which Affected Whittier's Career

We are here to honor a poet, not to dissect him. As sons and daughters of New England, we gather in the city of Whittier's birth to remind ourselves not so much what was mortal in him as to what was immortal.

It is a sort of a family gathering. Whittier was our poet—the poet of the Merrimac River and these low-lying hills, the singer of hearthside and countryside in Massachusetts. We recall him with the affection and pride of kinsmen. Many things that need to be said of him in other gatherings, among different surroundings, do not need to be said here.

We New Englanders knew Whittier "in his habit as he lived." He did not dwell apart in some ivory tower of the imagination, sheltered and secluded from his fellow men. He was a plain, homely citizen of this commonwealth, farmer, editor, member of the legislature; he went to church, went to the post office, [and] went to the polls, precisely like the rest of us. He was a good neighbor, and he had the happiness of saying, toward the close of his career, that he never lost a friend.

Modest, Brave and Gentle[8]

Whittier's life was an open book: all New England, all the world, could read it. He was a shrewd, versatile Yankee, with a knack of getting things done; done in this way, if practicable, if not, in the best way possible under the circumstances—a Yankee trait, by the way, which he shared with a frontier politician named Lincoln. Like Lincoln, Whittier was modest, brave, and gentle. His only harshness was in the severity of his speech toward the slaveholder, and he apologized for this by quoting Garrison's remark that "It was a waste of politeness to be courteous to the devil."

Like Lincoln, Whittier was rustic, provincial—the stuff out of which the best cosmopolites are made. He was a man primarily of his place and time; and both place and time were good. He was born in a Massachusetts farmhouse, and in an hour when the great humanitarian ideals of the eighteenth century were still pouring their generous flood into the nineteenth. "My father," Whittier said proudly, "was an old-fashioned Democrat, and really believed in the Preamble to the Bill of Rights which reaffirmed the Declaration of Independence."

In this then secluded valley of the Merrimac the Quaker boy felt the pulse of that European movement of emancipation,

The Merrimac River on Pleasant Valley Road in Amesbury where Whittier took walks

which has transformed, and is still transforming our modern world. When we recall the isolation, the poverty, the disadvantages of Whittier's boyhood, we must not forget that he had, after all, the best education that any boy can have, namely, the company of a few big ideas.

There are times and circumstances, of course, where it is proper and instructive to dwell upon Whittier's limitations. It is the task of biography and criticism to make these limitations clear. He lacked, for example, natural robustness of body; his physical endowment was impoverished; he would have been a happier man, and probably his poetry would have been richer, had he known a more full-blooded life of the senses.

Limited in his physical capacity to perceive beauty,[9] he was also limited in his artistic power to interpret it. His poetry is deficient in sensuous charm. Its passion is a moral passion only. Gifted with a natural facility in meter and rhyme, he was nevertheless a careless workman. His ear was not delicate, his rhymes were often slovenly, his style was frequently diffuse and repetitious, he wrote far too much. He had little reverence for craftsmanship, he spoke with a

kind of contempt of "literary reputation." As compared with the kingly poets of all the ages, the poet whom we love and celebrate today is but the master of a province only.

All this, and more than this, will be said from time to time by the voice of literary criticism. It is inevitable, and it is desirable, that that voice should be heard. Each generation must make its own assessment of its inherited literary property. But whatever may be said by technical criticism, either now or later, this anniversary hour in Haverhill is neither the time nor the place for it. We do not meet as critics, but as grateful admirers of a figure beloved and benign. And it may be well to recall the couplet which an eighteenth century verse-maker, disquieted at foolish criticism, composed:

> The critics are the greatest race of men:
> The hyper-critics are as great again.

Some criticism of Whittier has been hyper-criticism; over-clever and under-informed; ill-acquainted with the man with his times and with the nature of his task.

His Noble Qualities

You who know your Whittier will allow me to mention the noble qualities which he admittedly possessed, and which may appropriately be brought to mind today.

First, he had Vision. He was a Seer, not merely a Singer. His eyes had been opened. A great astronomer once declared that he had swept the whole heavens with his glass and had seen no God; but to Emerson, a poet—a Seer—that small sky was "full of light and deity." Whittier, like Emerson, gazed into the unseen. He saw behind the veil of fact and form. When he first read Burns, how fresh the world revealed itself to his boyish eyes:

> New light on home-see
> Nature beamed,
> New glory over woman;
> And daily life and duty seemed
> No longer poor and common
>
> . . . . .
>
> Why dreams of lands of gold on pearl
> Of loving knight and lady
> When farmer boy and barefoot girl
> Were wandering there already?

He saw the world as it is, with romance underlying all familiar things. Before his vision rose the past of New England, rich in local history and legend. He wrote ballads about Indian and Puritan, Quaker and sea-captain. These vanished scenes of colonial New England lived again in his revivifying fancy; and Milton, Burke, and Byron were his guides to the older world across the sea.

But his imagination did not linger there. His vision penetrated to the heart of those present issues which perplexed his countrymen in the thirty years that preceded the Civil War. He saw amid all the confusion and crosscurrents of opinion, the straight line of right and wrong. He knew men. He was the keenest politician in Essex County. He felt the agony of that crisis when our

> dismal Massachusetts ice
> Burned more than other's fire.

Born a poet, his mind was nevertheless formed, his imagination was kindled, and his hand was perfected, amid the fiery pressure of events. He voiced not only the romance of those silent generation of pioneers from whom he sprang, but also the

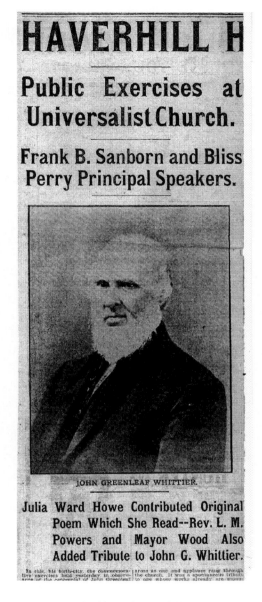

HAVERHILL H

Public Exercises at Universalist Church.

Frank B. Sanborn and Bliss Perry Principal Speakers.

JOHN GREENLEAF WHITTIER.

Julia Ward Howe Contributed Original Poem Which She Read--Rev. L. M. Powers and Mayor Wood Also Added Tribute to John G. Whittier.

Newspaper headline of Haverhill Centennial

29

THE POET'S BIRTHPLACE AND THE BUTTONWOODS, THE HOME OF THE HAVERHILL HISTORICAL SOCIETY, WILL BE OPEN DURING THE DAY.

THERE WILL BE AN EXHIBIT OF WHITTIER'S MANUSCRIPTS AND FIRST EDITIONS AT THE PUBLIC LIBRARY, SUMMER STREET.

Centennial Announcement

dumb passion of sympathy, of indignation, which was to swing vast armies of common men into march and battle.

A Man of Vision

He saw that moral problems were the real problems. With the veracity and boldness of the Seers and Prophets of old, Whittier cried "Thus saith the Lord," and men believed him. To him the enduring verities were no mere form of words. Like Lowell, he held that "The Ten Commandments will not budge." He did not attempt to restate any of the eternal truths; he applied them. He did not create new beliefs and emotions; he rested back upon the old faiths and hopes of humanity, he was borne upward and onward by them, like a swimmer who yields himself to the surf.

Hence, his vision of the future; his sense of the continuity and unity of human life; his faith that its discords will be hushed in some ultimate peace. You cannot defeat such a man. In one of the darkest hours of the Anti-Slavery conflict Whittier was writing in "Barclay of Ury:"

> Happy he whose inward ear
> Angel comfortings can hear,
> O'er the rabble's laughter;
> And while Hatred's fagots burn,
> Glimpses through the smoke discern
> Of the good hereafter.
>
> . . . . .
>
> Thus, with somewhat of the Seer,
> Must the moral pioneer
> From the Future borrow;
> Clothe the waste with dreams of grain,
> And, on midnight's sky of rain,
> Paint the golden morrow!

A Man of Loyalty

Whittier was not only a man of Vision; he was also a man of Loyalty. He was loyal to the town where he was born. To the very end, he loved the farm where he had toiled in youth, the desk on which he wrote his early verses, the

Quaker habit of saying "thee" and "thy." It used to be charged against Thomas Jefferson, after his return from France, that he had "eschewed his native victuals." Whittier remained innocent of this transgression. One likes his loyalty even in the little things: for fifty years he ordered his coat from the same tailor, his boots from the same boot-maker. That the boot-maker went back to his native Paris after awhile, made no difference to Whittier; during the rest of his life he simply ordered the boots from Paris, from the same workman. The fact is trivial, but it shows the man. He was faithful to old associations, however humble.

He was rooted in this soil of ours: he was a Haverhill man, an Amesbury man, an Essex County man, a Massachusetts man. His local sentiment rings true. He loved the names of Newbury, Ipswich and Wenham, of Andover, Salem and Boston. How glowingly he calls the roll of the counties of the Bay State in his "Massachusetts to Virginia"!

How completely did this local loyalty become transfigured into sectional loyalty! What a spokesman for New England he was for forty years! And when at last the nation stood where New England and that newer New England of the West had long been standing, how resonant was the note of national loyalty that rang in Whittier's "Barbara Frietchie," in "Laus Deo," and in the "Centennial Hymn."

His loyalties of fireside, of township and county, of state and section are all in tune with his Americanism, like bells within bells chiming consonant music. And his Americanism in turn is keyed to a still nobler loyalty, — I mean his loyalty of the wider interests of mankind.

"America" is a magnificent word, but a better one still is the word "civilization." Let me quote to you the definition of a civilization, given in a single sentence by an Irishman, the late Lord Russell of Killowen, before the American Bar Association:

> It's true signs are thought for the poor and suffering, chivalrous regard and respect for woman, the frank recognition of human brotherhood, irrespective of race or color or nation or religion; the narrowing of the domain of mere force as a governing factor in the world, the love of ordered freedom, abhorrence of what is mean and cruel and vile, ceaseless devotion to the claims of justice.

That is a great jurist's definition of human progress, but it might have been written to describe the spirit of Whittier's poetry. He kept, to the end, his boyhood's faith in Man. Partisan as he was, and patriotic American as he was, he was loyal to a still higher citizenship. He could say with his friend Garrison: "Our country is the World — our countrymen are mankind."

Message for Today

I have said that Whittier was a man of Vision and of Loyalty. Have we outgrown him? Aside from that local sentiment which has brought us here to honor his memory, do we recognize that his poetry still has a message for today? It happens that upon at least two of the issues immediately before the American people, Whittier's verse takes radical and

31

uncompromising ground, and that upon both of these issues one may safely venture the assertion that Whittier is absolutely and everlastingly right.

The real question is the first. Not, of course, the old issue of slavery. Not the wisdom or unwisdom of that hasty Reconstruction legislation when partisan advantage was inextricably confused with the ideal interests of former slaves.

A Worldwide Problem

The race question transcends any academic inquiry as to what ought to have been done in 1866. It affects the North, as well as the South, it touches the daily life of all of our citizens, industrially, politically, humanly. It molds the child's conception of Democracy. It tests the faith of the adult. It is by no means an American problem only.

The relation of the white with the yellow and black races is an urgent question all around the globe. The present unrest in India, the struggle between Japan and Russia, the national reconstruction of China, the sensitiveness of both Canadian and Californian to Oriental immigration, are impressive signs that the adjustment of race differences is the greatest humanitarian task now confronting the world.

What is going on in our own states, North and South, is only a local phase of a world problem. Now Whittier's opinions upon that world problem are unmistakable. He believed, quite literally, that all men are brothers; that oppression of one man or one race degrades the whole human family; and that there should be fullest equality of opportunity. That a mere difference in color should close the door of civil, industrial and political hope upon any individual was a hateful thing

to the Quaker poet. The whole body of his verse is a protest against the assertion of race pride, against the emphasis upon racial differences.

To Whittier there was no such thing as a "white man's civilization." The only distinction was between civilization and Barbarism. He had faith in education, in equality before the law, in freedom of opportunity and in the ultimate triumph of brotherhood. This faith is at once too sentimental and too dogmatic to suit those persons who have exalted economic efficiency into a fetish, and who have talked loudly at times—though rather less loudly since the Russo-Japanese war—about the white man's task of governing the backward races. But whatever progress has been made by the American Negro since the Civil War, in self-respect, in moral and intellectual development and—for that matter—in economic efficiency, has been due to fidelity to those principles which Whittier and other like-minded men and women long ago enunciated. The immense tasks which still remain, alike for "higher" as for "lower" races, can be worked out by following Whittier's programme, if they can be worked out at all.

The Great Hope of Peace

The second of the immediate issues upon which Whittier's voice is clear is that of international peace. Though the burdens of militarism were far less apparent sixty years ago than they are today, and the necessity of allaying race-conflicts by peaceful means far less instant, Whittier belonged to the little band of agitators for peace.

Read his lines on the Peace Convention in Brussels in 1848. Then, as now, there were faithless critics to point out the folly of this dream of disarmament. Whittier states their case, more skillfully than they could do it for themselves; then he brushes it aside, and in assured vision foretells the day of ultimate international good will. To him it is 'The great hope resting on the truth of God.' But it rests, and does not waver.

And Time is justifying the poet's faith. The faithful few who journeyed to Brussels at their own charges and upon their own initiative in 1848, have given place in 1907 to the duly accredited representatives of forty-two powers, representing the whole territory of the globe. But these professional diplomatists, warriors and lawyers who have been meeting at The Hague are not in advance of,

and many of them are far behind, the sentiment of the common people whom they represent. The popular dissatisfaction with the concrete results of the last Hague conference is the best proof of the real progress of the cause with which Whittier was identified.

Let us think of him, therefore, not as a mere combatant, but as a victor. The causes for which he battled were noble causes, and they are noble causes still. But he has passed, and indeed he passed long before his bodily death, into that more quiet air, that ampler light, where the voices of controversy are hushed, and where the face of Eternal Beauty is unshadowed and serene.

The evening newspaper with highlights of the events in Haverhill and Amesbury

33

NEWBURYPORT

The Historical Society of Old Newbury hosted the local Centennial observance at a gathering at the Whitefield Church on State Street.[10] The speaker was William Lloyd Garrison, Jr., son of the noted abolitionist, a native son.

It was in Garrison's *Free Press* in Newburyport where Whittier's poems were first published. Later his political and antislavery work, as well as friendships, strengthened his connections to Newburyport and its neighboring towns.

Socially, he enjoyed an annual event known as "The Laurels," hosted by William Ashby and held in June near the Merrimac River when the mountain laurel were in bloom. He penned some of his local poetry for these occasions. "To William Ashby and His Household" was written for the last one, and some of the stanzas were incorporated into "The Laurels."

As with other Centennial observances, the music selected for the program used poems written by Whittier. Letters were read from noted guests who were unable to attend: Mrs. Gertrude Whittier Cartland of Newburyport, Whittier's cousin; Thomas Wentworth Higginson, former local minister of the First Religious Society (Unitarian), an abolitionist and Whittier biographer; and the Honorable Albert E. Pillsbury, former Massachusetts Attorney General, 1891–94.

Programme.

ORGAN PRELUDE

Miss Ruth Titcomb

SINGING ....Tune, "Manvah," Page 216

Audience

The harp at Nature's advent strung,
  Has never ceased to play:
The song the stars of morning sung
  Has never died away.

And prayer is made, and praise is given
  By all things near and far:
The ocean looketh up to heaven
  And mirrors every star:

The green earth sends her incense up
  From many a mountain shrine;
From folded leaf and dewy cup
  She pours her sacred wine.

The blue sky is the temple's arch
  Its transept, earth and air:
The music of its starry march
  The chorus of a prayer.

So nature keeps the reverent frame
  With which her years began:
And all her signs and voices shame
  The prayerless heart of man.

SOLO—"The Eternal Goodness" ....Hawley

C. Wilson Stanwood.

COMMEMORATIVE EXERCISES

READING OF LETTERS
> Grace Carleton Moody

SOLO—"All as God Wills" ....Silsby
> Edith Russell Wills

ADDRESS
> Wm. Lloyd Garrison

SOLO—"Hope of the Ages" ....Lidelle
> C. Wilson Stanwood.

SINGING
> Audience

Oh sometimes gleams upon our sight
Through present wrong the Eternal Right.
And step by step, since Time began,
We see the steady gain of man.

That all of good the past hath had
Remains to make our own time glad,
Our common, daily life divine,
And every land a Palestine.

Through the harsh noises of the day
A low, sweet prelude finds its way:
Through clouds of doubt, and creeds of fear
A light is breaking, calm and clear

Henceforth my heart shall sigh no more
For olden time and holier shore:
God's love and blessing, then and there,
Are now and here and everywhere.

Historical Society of Old Newbury

Exercises Commemorating the
Anniversary of the Birth of

John Greenleaf Whittier

At the Whitefield Church, Newburyport, December seventeenth,
nineteen hundred seven, at seven
forty-five o'clock.

====================================

LETTERS FROM NOTABLE CITIZENS

PRINTED IN THE CENTENNIAL PROGRAM

---

29 BUCKINGHAM STREET,
CAMBRIDGE, Dec. 15, 1907.

REV. H. E. LOMBARD:

Dear Sir:—Returning home after a hurried and busy absence, chiefly on Whittier business, I find your letter which had been mislaid. I had no conception of the wide and eager interest that would be felt all over the country in respect to this Whittier commemoration; it is even greater than that called forth by the Centennial celebration of the birth of Longfellow, which was so interesting and impressive in Cambridge. I count it a great joy and honor to be one of the oldest of those who can testify to the earlier years of Whittier's life and to the genuineness and simplicity which always marked it, growing only stronger and maturer as years went on.

It seems to me most appropriate that there should be these three parallel commemorations of him, as it were—at Haverhill, Amesbury and Newburyport—and only regret that it is thought wiser for me to forbear taking closer part in the tributes which are to be paid to him in a region of the country with which I have so many happy associations. I am, sir,

Yours very cordially,

THOMAS WENTWORTH HIGGINSON.

COMMEMORATIVE EXERCISES

REV. HERBERT E. LOMBARD:

Dear Sir:—It would give me great pleasure to attend the Newburyport Historical Society's commemoration of Whittier, but my engagements permit me only to thank you for this opportunity of adding a word to what may appropriately be said on his centennial anniversary. New England itself never produced, even in Benjamin Franklin, a more remarkable character than this Yankee Quaker, sage, saint, politician and poet. He lives and grows today with an increasing and permanent fame. For a considerable part of Whittier's life the leaders in literature, politics and society turned their backs upon him because he was an abolitionist and reformer. To those who remember that period, if they have any sense of humor, it is highly edifying to note the change of attitude toward him with the progress of time. The professors of English and other critical characters are now beginning to find out that Whittier was a great poet, and there even are signs that American writers of our history may in time discover, as the German Von Holst long ago did, that Whittier's fiery verse, with "Uncle Tom's Cabin" and the Biglow Papers, really played a larger part than many speeches, platforms or Acts of Congress in shaping the destiny of the country. If Whittier had written nothing but "The Pine Tree," "Snow-Bound," and "The Eternal Goodness," these three masterpieces would prove his title to rank with the highest in as many distinct realms of poetry. Apart from any question of his final place in literature, there is no other character in our annals who so much reminds us of Andrew Fletcher's pregnant saying, that he who can make the ballads of a nation need not care who make its laws. I suspect that among all his productions Whittier took most personal satisfaction in that flood of soul-stirring lyrics written in lines of battle and blazing with the wrath of all the Hebrew prophets, in which the "dough-races, dough heads and dough hearts" of the period of slavery and rebellion were shrivelled up and utterly consumed. (I borrow these epithets from Webster, though the passage does not sound much like the 7th of March speech.) Whittier has a recognized and growing claim upon the world at large for the homage due to all poets and seers. The American nation owes him a special, if not a higher debt, for his part in waking its conscience and bracing its resolve to the task of purification from slavery. In that day the pen of this militant Quaker was mightier than many swords.

Sincerely yours,

ALBERT E. PILLSBURY

BOSTON, Dec. 14, 1907.

———

108 FARMINGTON AVENUE, }
HARTFORD, CONN., Dec. 14, 1907. }

DEAR MR. LOMBARD:

I feel proud that my few weeks in Byfield each summer should entitle me, a Connecticut woman, to share in the happy occasion of honoring the memory of the most lovable of American poets.

The impressions of one who comes freshly each year to the Whittier country from other surroundings may also have a distinct value of their own.

Each August as I return the vision of river, of marsh, and distant sea bring to my mind exquisite soul-revealing lines from Whittier's poems discriptive of the scenes that he loved and the whole atmosphere seems permeated with the influence of his simple and beautiful life. His white personality of strong and pure manhood seems to be still an abiding presence and is expressed in his deeper poems which reveal thoughts which have the Christ-like quality of healing not only for the individual but for the nation.

I cannot tell you how often memories of those simple rooms at Amesbury, especially the garden room, and the poet's bedroom, come to my mind.

In these days when there is so much talk of the simple life and at the same time such restless unremitting effort to grow rich quickly, when old standards of integrity seem so often replaced by those of doubtful honor, men like Whittier and Emerson whose standard was "plain living and high thinking," seem to stand out like statues of iron against a background of gray compromise.

The house where they lived and all of their environment seem also to utter not so much a protest as tender expressions of regret that so many in modern life miss happiness in the struggle to attain only what this world can give, and lose the capacity to enjoy those supreme things of human life which this world can neither give nor take away.

Thanking you for this opportunity to express my appreciation. Believe me,

Most cordially yours,

EMILY M. MORGAN.

---

250 NEWBURY STREET,
BOSTON, December 14, 1907,

REV. HERBERT E. LOMBARD:

President of the Historical Society of Old Newbury,

My Dear Mr. Lombard:—Miss Scudder and I have received your letter in regard to the centenary of Whittier's birth, and our thoughts will be with you and the people of Old Newbury on the evening of the seventeenth.

We love to think that something more than chance led our little community of women to South Byfield, some drawing of the Spirit, perhaps, that sweet country-side, beloved by the Apostle of Simplicity. It is good to remember that he, too, walked in the lanes we know so well, and watched the tidal river wind noisily through the marshes in the sunset. And even as the Lake County in England seems visibly to interpret the spirit of Wordsworth, so surely, the peaceful strength of the country around Adelynrood, its rugged hillocks and sweeping salt meadows, its wide skies and pungent sea-breath, may interpret to us the Quaker Poet.

Very sincerely yours,

VIDA D. SCUDDER,
FLORENCE CONVERSE.

Son of Abolitionist Gives Tribute to Whittier

William Lloyd Garrison, Jr., was nearly seventy years old, a retired successful businessman in the wool trade and securities investments, and a social reformer in his own right. Growing up during the social and political upheavals of the Abolitionist movement, he had not been isolated from the pre–Civil War struggles. He witnessed first the public's persecution and ostracism of his father, and later the hero worship as the movement succeeded.

William Lloyd Garrison, Jr.

Garrison's character was obviously strengthened by the lessons from his parents and, as an adult, he championed many reforms, including women's suffrage, the rights of African Americans, and the cause of Ireland.[11]

A local newspaper clipping stated the sentiments of those who attended the Centennial celebration:

> ...it was gratifying to all present as well as singularly appropriate that the address of the occasion should be delivered by William Lloyd Garrison, whose father was so closely identified with Whittier in the anti-slavery movement.

GARRISON'S ADDRESS

Among the papers left by my father was a penciled tribute to Whittier, spoken at Newburyport, February, 1865, which I believe has never appeared in print. From it I extract this allusion to his first meeting with the poet:

> Nearly thirty-nine years ago, in the early flush and romance of youth, we became acquainted with each other—I an incipient newspaper editor, and he a diffident lad on his shoemaker's bench, timidly venturing now and then to send an anonymous effusion to the press, to which his imagination gave birth, while his hands were busy with the lapstone and the last.
>
> The chain of our friendship has remained bright and enduring from that hour to this, nor do I believe that either time or eternity will be able to sunder it. Espousing the Anti-Slavery cause almost simultaneously with myself, he has unflinchingly stood by it through every form of temptation and trial, and given to it an inspiration and power beyond that of any living man. His melting appeals and clarion notes, expressed in most felicitous verse, reached the home of refinement and the fisherman's hut in every part of New England, and penetrated 'every cabin and beyond the mountains'—giving to the speech of the lecturing advocate an electric influence, and swaying even the most disorderly gatherings with magical potency. They have touched and moulded millions of hearts, and mightily helped to break millions of fetters; and without them, in all probability, there had been no jubilee for us to celebrate tonight.[12]

Whoever else may be remembered or forgotten in this great struggle, the name of John Greenleaf Whittier will be placed among the foremost of the champions of universal freedom and the benefactors of mankind, and shine in the historic heavens a star of the first magnitude. God bless him abundantly and forever!

When preparing a lecture on Whittier to be delivered in Newburyport, in 1859, Mr. Garrison wrote to his subject, asking for data concerning his life. In sending it, Whittier wrote:

> Do me, as I am sure thou wilt, the justice to note that I have not lived merely for literary reputation,—that what I most desired was to do my duty as a man, all else was incidental and subordinate.—I hope thee will not edify the Newburyport folks with any extended recitations of my "first things." I don't think they are worth reviving.

Matthew Arnold, in his essay on Wordsworth, declares that "poetry is nothing less than the most perfect speech of man, that in which he comes nearest to being able to utter the truth." And Lowell describes poesy as "the true preacher of the word," and defender of the flock in times of danger and trouble "when the established shepherds have thrown down their crooks and fled.—From her white breasts flows the strong milk which nurses our patriots and martyrs. She robs the fires of heat, makes the axe edgeless and dignifies the pillory and the gallows. She is the great reformer, and where the love of her is strong and healthy, wickedness and wrong cannot prevail.

In treating of Whittier tonight, I shall confine myself to this phase of his poetry, consecrated to anti-slavery and reform,

William Lloyd Garrison, Sr.

taking for my theme "The Poet of Freedom."

Whittier's Heritage

The biographer of a great life dwells naturally on the origin and ancestry of his subject. So fully is he persuaded that individual traits and virtues are evolved and are not sporadic, that he searches for the root from which they ought to grow.

It is not so difficult to find in Whittier's descent some claim to exceptional qualities, for from his Puritan ancestor on the maternal side, Rev. Stephen Bachelor, the first minister of Hampton, N.H., came also Daniel Webster, and other men of note, bearing the characteristic deep-set and remarkable eyes in evidence of succession. And, on the father's side, the Huguenot Greenleafs, or Feuilleverts, were a sturdy and notable stock, although none of special distinction preceded the Quaker poet.

Not unnaturally, therefore, the Haverhill boy found in himself the impulse of poetry; and, although the hindrances to its expression were from circumstances severe, as surely as his native Merrimac sought the sea, so must his muse find a public.

The Haverhill farm house where Whittier was born and passed his boyhood, survives with little change. The rugged region and unwilling soil suggest the hardship of a subsistence wrung from such unpromising material. The isolation of the home, with no neighbors in sight, offered small chance of companionship in week days, whatever the silence of Friends' meeting on Sundays may have furnished. The meagre supply of books in the household was insufficient for the famished mind.

These early conditions contrast vividly with those of Lowell, Whittier's companion anti-slavery poet, who, like Holmes, Emerson and Longfellow, was cradled in ease and amid cultured surroundings, entering upon the world's broad threshold with the advantage of an academic stamp. Perhaps to Whittier his great good fortune was to miss these accessories. Who knows what loss might in his case have offset such gain, or what refinement of scholarship might have done to weaken the vigor of his service to freedom?

It would be difficult to find on the earth's surface a concentration of more diversified industry than is included in the small county of Essex, in Massachusetts. At Lawrence, the great centre of cotton and woolen industries, the Merrimac river, changing its beauty into use, enters into servitude and turns the busy mill wheels with its gigantic power.

From Gloucester and Marblehead and Swampscott the hardy fishermen go out to the Banks, while the hungry sea exacts its yearly tribute of human life, leaving in evidence its pathetic legacy of widows and orphans. In Lynn and Haverhill the modern shoe factory has made obsolete the ancient shop and bench. From Salem and Newburyport sailed, in the days we are considering, the merchant vessels that brought back the wealth to build those rare mansions which today suggest an atmosphere of home and comfort, unequalled by the newer and pretentious dwellings now in vogue.

Commerce was honorable then, and to trade in the East Indies was not considered unpatriotic, nor were merchants a dangerous class of men. We have changed all that, and, while the tides still flow and the watery pathway around the globe continues open to all keels, the wharves of Essex county exist chiefly as monuments of former greatness.

Outside of the great towns the farmer still tills the earth, onions find the soil of Marblehead congenial, the salt marshes, those "low, green prairies of the sea," yield up their annual crop of salt hay, and a new industry, confined by nature to the "home market," brings every summer its pleasure and rest-seeking crowd of visitors.

So Whittier was by birthright the poet of the farmer, the fisherman, the shoemaker and the mechanic, and who shall say that he was trained in a bad university for his vocation?

The inspiration of the Scottish poet, whose volume came by accident into his boyish hands, he has himself described, when, in the harvest time he "sought the maple's shadow" and sang with Burns the hours away.

> I matched with Scotland's heathery hills
>   The sweetbriar and the clover;
> With Ayr and Doon, my native rills,
>   Their wood hymns chanting over.

It was a time not far removed from

Indian warfare, and the tales of the dusky people who had been driven from their homes and hunting grounds, were neighborhood themes. To these were joined the stories of witchcraft and supernatural occurrences, and the imagination of the youth repeopled the region and embalmed in verse their legends, as Irving did in happiest prose the Dutch traditions of the Hudson.

Illustration of Whittier's schoolhouse

The familiar story of Whittier's first success in gaining an audience, through the verses secretly sent by his appreciative sister to the *Newburyport Free Press*, the cordial recognition of their merit by the young editor, and his request for more, the author's joy at first seeing them in print, and the subsequent visit of the editor to Haverhill, on discovering the identity of his shy contributor, to commend and encourage him, have been fully described by both participants, and brought to public notice on each recurrent birthday of the poet's later years.

It was a fortunate conjunction of personalities, not more for American poetry than for the anti-slavery reform. Henceforth the one was to be yoked in service to the other. The slave had found a minstrel who would sing the story of his woe and outrage into souls impervious to ordinary speech. The all-pervading and seemingly impregnable system of oppression was soon to hear the bugle call for its unconditional surrender.

"Poetry will not give him bread," said the practical father. Truly not for long years to come. But the consciousness of the gift opened the way for new ambitions and stimulated the boy's desire for education. We see him drop the farm work for the advantage of two brief seasons at the village academy, sewing shoes and teaching school between the sessions, for his support. The resources of the little town soon failing to satisfy his growing needs, he sought the larger opportunities of the great city, and naturally found his occupation in the congenial pursuits of journalism. Even there his literary strivings must be subordinated to the drudgery of newspaper work and the unpoetic advocacy of the gospel of protection. His uninspired pen turned off editorials for the Boston Manufacturer, in behalf of the infant industries of the country, which in his venerable age he was destined to see still clamoring for the nurse's bottle. Singularly enough he never abated his faith in the system which, after sixty years of additional trial, had not imparted sufficient strength for the infants to walk alone.

The magnet that drew him back to Haverhill was not the attraction of the farm, but the Essex Gazette, which he edited for a few months, and then responded to a call from Hartford, to take charge of the *New England Weekly Review*, during the temporary absence of its editor, the famous George D. Prentice. "I could not have been more utterly astonished," he afterward wrote, "if I had been told that I was appointed prime minister to the Khan of Tartary."

"The firstlings of his muse" were now sufficient for a volume, which he published in 1831, the year of *The Liberator's* beginning, under the title of "Legends of New England," written in verse and prose, which, although indicative of promise, contained little of permanent value.

1833 — A Turning Point

Mr. Garrison, whose admiration for Whittier and whose unalterable belief in his success were outspoken, was evidently impatient for the poet to harness his muse to the chariot of reform. "Can we not induce him to devote his brilliant genius more to the advancement of our cause and kindred enterprises, and less to the creations of romance and fancy, and the disturbing influences of political strife?" he writes to friends in Haverhill. But the die was already cast, and the year 1833, when this was written, was to mark the entire surrender of Whittier's life to the slave's cause.

The decision was announced by his treatise on "Justice and Expediency; or Slavery considered with a view to its Rightful or Effectual Remedy, Abolition."

Poor as he was, Whittier published the pamphlet at his own expense, and the joy of Mr. Garrison may be imagined on receiving a copy of it in England, where he was then laboring to enlist British sympathy and assistance.

It was a year memorable in the annuals of the anti-slavery movement. Lydia Maria Child, sacrificing her immediate literary reputation on the altar of freedom, published her brave "Appeal in favor of that class of Americans called Africans." If Whittier surrendered his prospects for political success by adherence to abolition, not less did Mrs. Child abandon, without regret, her growing popularity, and face the social indignities that were to come. As she says later, "Old dreams vanished, old associates departed, and all things became new."

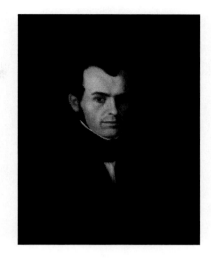

Whittier, 1833

More important events were yet to happen, before the year was ended. In December, delegates were chosen to the convention in Philadelphia which was to establish the American Anti-Slavery Society. Among them was Whittier, unable to bear the expenses of the journey, and aided by his noble friend, Samuel E. Sewall.

It was an extraordinary occasion, and its historical importance was impressed upon the minds of the participants. The famous "Declaration of Sentiments," which was to supplement and make effective the Declaration of Independence, was presented to the convention with impressive dignity. As Whittier records it, "One after another passed up to the platform, signed, and retired in silence. All felt the deep responsibility of the occasion:—the shadow and forecast of a life-long struggle rested upon every countenance."

Thirty years afterward he testified to his appreciation of the honor which he was permitted to share. In the light of experience he could write:

47

I am not insensible to literary reputation; I love, perhaps too well, the praise and good will of my fellowmen; but I set a higher value on my name as appended to the Anti-Slavery Declaration of 1833 than on the title page of any book.

Of the three-score signers of the Declaration, he was destined to be the last survivor but one,—the venerable Robert Purvis, of Philadelphia.

The period of trial was now at hand. The poet had heard the mandate:

Forego thy dreams of lettered ease,
Put thou the scholar's promise by,
The rights of man are more than these.
He heard and answered: 'Here am I.'

It needs the graphic, resurrecting pen of a Carlyle to make relive in briefest space the thirty years of storm and stress which were to follow; years of obloquy and persecution, of great reputations destroyed, of obscure men and women exalted, of fierce discussion, of "irrepressible conflict" of humiliating slave-hunts, of public sentiment awakened

. . . . .

to the higher aims
Of a land that has lost for a little her lust for
gold,
And love of peace that was full of
wrongs and shames,
Horrible, hateful, monstrous, not to be
told;

of Southern arrogance and Northern subservience, of Sumter's downfall, of the "uprising of a great people," of a nation in arms, of a holocaust of human lives, and of the emancipation of a race. Theme more inspiring for an Iliad than any petty siege of Troy, and waiting for its Homer. And of this world-moving story Whittier could-have truthfully written, "All of which I saw and part of which I was."

In no crisis of the conflict do you miss his voice, and what is more, the man behind the voice.

O, poet of past deeds of valor, easy is it to sit in safety, and, amidst applause, to tell of times that tried men's souls! But, to be one's self in the battle's forefront, to sing in unstudied strains in the conflict's intervals the hope and faith of Truth crushed, yet triumphant, to sound the challenge but never the retreat, this is indeed to realize the ideal and doubly to hallow the divine gift. How few the poets who could write over their poems on contemporaneous subjects,

Yet here at least an earnest sense
Of human right and weal is shown;
A hate of tyranny intense,
And hearty in its vehemence,
As if my brother's pain and sorrow were
my own.

Throughout the long and discouraging conflict of opinion, Whittier is to be seen in the anti-slavery van. Differences of method sometimes separated him from his old companions, but the breach was temporary and when the attack was ordered the ranks closed up. His garb and principles of peace did not exempt him from mobs. After rough treatment by an excited populace in Concord, N. H. in company with his friend George Thompson, the eloquent English abolitionist, he was forced to seek safety in flight. Two months later, in Boston, in the autumn of the same year, the "gentlemen of property and standing" combined to lay violent hands on Thompson, and, missing him, to assault and imprison the editor of *The Liberator*.

At the grated window of Garrison's cell in Leverett street jail, on the evening of the eventful day, with Samuel J. May and Bronson Alcott, Whittier offered his

Pennsylvania Hall before and during the fire - 1838

words of sympathy, and declined the facetious invitation of the happy prisoner to come in and pass the night. The mob little dreamed that it was adding to the persecuted abolitionists such powerful recruits as Wendell Phillips and Charles Sumner.

By the light of Pennsylvania Hall, in Philadelphia, dedicated to the services of freedom, and fired by incendiary rioters, the figure of the anti-slavery poet is revealed, in the vivid midnight glare, watching the destruction of his office in the building, in company with the great men and women of the cause.

With him stood the Grimke sisters, "Carolina's high-souled daughters," who had liberated their slaves and were helping not only to free the colored race, but to emancipate their own sex. Their mission was to wage a double battle full of peril and pathos. Assailed by the Pastoral Letter of the Massachusetts Congregational churches, how valiantly Whittier defended them with his indignant verse!

O, ever may the power which led
  Their way to such a fiery trial,
And strengthened womanhood to tread
  The wine-press of such self-denial,
Be round them in an evil land,

With wisdom and with strength from Heaven,
With Miriam's voice, and Judith's hand
And Deborah's song, for triumph given.

Virginia claimed George Latimer [escaped slave][13] as a chattel, hoping to drag him into servitude again, but the Fugitive Slave Law was not yet and the merciful court prevented. How electrifying then rang Whittier's grand defiance of Massachusetts to Virginia:

Thank God, not yet so vilely can
  Massachusetts bow;
The spirit of her early time is with her even
  now;
Deem not because the Pilgrim blood move
  slow, and calm and cool,
She thus can stoop her chainless neck, a
  sister's slave and tool.

Whittier Denounces Daniel Webster

But darker days of humiliation were to come. Daniel Webster, the idol of Massachusetts, was to mark still further the subservience of the North. The great hopes for freedom which his earlier speech at Plymouth Rock had inspired,were dashed by the dreaded utterance of the seventh of March, in 1850.

The popular press and pulpit bowed subservient to the great man. Here and there a lone minister, like Theodore Parker, lifted his voice of protest and warning and a few unpopular newspapers arraigned the sin and sinner. But it was reserved for Whittier to concentrate in one brief poem the terrible judgment of posterity.

The poet himself had been one of the statesman's strong admirers, hoping against hope that he would redeem his earlier promise. When the fateful hour struck and faith was dispelled, came the sad, pathetic, scathing verses of "Ichabod," rivalled only by Browning's "Lost Leader," and destined to survive in literature with Webster's memory:

> O, dumb be passion's stormy rage
>   When he who might
> Have lighted up and led the age,
>   Falls back in night.
>
> Of all we loved and honored, naught
>   Save power remains, —
> A Fallen angel's pride of thought,
>   Still strong in chains.
>
> All else is gone from those great eyes
>   The soul has fled;
> When faith is lost, when honor dies,
>   The man is dead.

Illustration used on the 1837 broadside publication of Whittier's poem "Our Countryman in Chains"

Daniel Webster

The fruits of Webster's apostasy soon ripened. Everywhere was seen the fugitive slaves who had sought shelter in the North flying to Canada, or hiding in terror from the prowling kidnapper. The rendition of [slave] Anthony Burns brought out the fire and force of Whittier, as he records the universal shame.

> And as I thought of Liberty
> Marched handcuffed down that sworded
>   street,
> The solid earth beneath my feet
> Reeled fluid as the sea.

And he invokes Massachusetts:

> "Mother of Freedom, wise and broad,
>   Rise awful in they strength," I said;
> Ah me, I spake but to the dead;
>   I stood upon her grave.

From this despairing mood the passage of the Personal Liberty Law relieved him, and how prompt he was to change the note to gladness.

> I said I stood upon thy grave,
>   My Mother State, when last the moon
>   Of blossoms clomb the skies of June.
> Once more thy strong maternal arms
>   Are round about thy children flun
>   A lioness that guards her young.

50

The fast crowding events inspired always the poet's word. The Kansas emigrants from New England could sing his lines as they travelled across the prairie.

> We go to rear a wall of men
>   On Freedom's southern line,
> And plant beside the cotton tree
>   The rugged Northern pine.

It would be difficult to overrate the sustaining strength which the active laborers in the anti-slavery vineyard gained from the lyrical and impassioned poetry of Whittier and Lowell. How many a wearied speaker found his way to the attention and hearts of his hearers through an aptly quoted verse! At humble hearthstones where, as in all reforms, abolition first found its ardent disciples, what joy came into the household with a new poem from the anti-slavery bard! Faith, self-surrender, reliance upon principles, and religious elevation offset the depressing influences of neighborhood coldness and social disregard.

To have in crucial times the rhythmic consolation of Whittier, the eloquence of Phillips, and the prophetic editorials of *The Liberator*, was a compensation that made conventional society seem poor and pale in comparison. In the Lord's service

. . . . .

> better fire-walled Hell with Him
> Than golden-gated Paradise without.

Harper's Ferry

The cumulative force of thirty years of anti-slavery agitation and of moral growth revealed itself at length in John Brown's attack on Harper's Ferry. It was the immediate precursor of the Civil War, startling the nation and forcing upon the abolitionists the unwelcome conviction that slavery was to be destroyed by force instead of by peaceful and moral means. They had ever protested against the use of weapons other than spiritual, and could not believe that even the madness of the South would tempt it to bring about its own destruction.

"The lesson of the hour is insurrection," announced Wendell Phillips in Brooklyn at Plymouth church. "Insurrection of thought always precedes the insurrection of arms." Whittier deprecated the means employed by Brown, and expressed the hope that

> Nevermore may yon Blue Ridge the
>   Northern rifles hear,
> Nor see the light of blazing homes flash on
>   the negro's spear,

little dreaming of the sights and sounds the Blue Ridge was to see and hear in the long years of war soon to be ushered in. Nowhere surged the fierce tide of battle more constantly than in the lovely valley of the Shenandoah.

The bursting of the war cloud at Sumter's fall transferred the conflict from the abolitionists to the soldiers of the Union. The cannon along the Potomac drowned the voices of the platform. The anti-slavery work of conversion was ended and the necessity of war was to compel the proclamation of President Lincoln, in obedience to the Philadelphia "Declaration of Sentiments" just thirty years before.

Who that remembers the dark days preceding the edict of emancipation, the disasters in the field and the gathering reactionary sentiment at the North which demanded peace at any price, can forget the invaluable service of the radical anti-slavery advocates? Not confident of public support,

Abraham Lincoln

O North and South
Its victims both
Can ye not cry
"Let slavery die."
And union find in freedom?

These thrilling words were put to music and sung in the Union camps along the Virginia line by the Hutchinsons, until the earnest singers were expelled by McClellan's order. But he was powerless to expel the song. The hymn was read aloud to the assembled cabinet and visibly affected Lincoln, doubtless hastening the day of liberty.[14]

doubtful and depressed, the sad faced man of destiny at Washington scanned the horizon anxiously for the signs of Northern unity. It would be hard to estimate the influence of Whittier's quick response in his grand hymn, "Ein Feste Burg."

The same pen that could put purpose into the heart of the President could also put words into the mouths of the lowly contraband. The freedmen within our lines in South Carolina learned from their Northern teachers' lips the "Song of the Negro Boatman," and from many a cabin came its familiar strains:

> We wait beneath the furnace blast
> The pangs of transformation;
> Not painlessly does God recast
> And mould anew the nation.

> Hot burns the fire
> When wrongs expire;
> Nor spares the hand
> That from the land
> Uproots the ancient evil.

> What gives the wheat fields blades of steel?
> What points the rebel cannon?
> What sets the roaring rabble's heel
> On the old star spangled pennon?

> What breaks the oath
> Of the men of the South?
> What whets the knife
> For the Union's life?
> Hark to the answer: Slavery.

> Then waste no time on lesser foes
> In strife unworthy freemen.
> God lifts today the veil, and shows
> The features of the demon.

> Oh, praise an' tanks! De Lord he come
> To set de people free;
> An massa tink it day ob doom
> An' we ob jubilee.

> De Lord dat heap de Red Sea waves
> He jus' as 'trong as den;
> He says de word; we las' night slaves
> Today de Lord's freemen.

> Rude seems the song; each swarthy face,
> Flame-lighted, ruder still;
> We start to think that hapless race
> Must shape our good or ill;

> That laws of changeless justice bind
> Oppressor with oppressed;
> And, close as sin and suffering joined,
> We march to Fate abreast.

At length the proclamation comes and the last hope of the rebellion fades. It turns the tide of battle, and Union victories are to follow fast. The military necessity has yet to be established in constitutional amendment; and on hearing the bells ring for the congressional passage of the resolution, Whittier breaks into the exultation of "Laus Deo."

> It is done!
> Clang of bell and roar of gun
> Send the tidings up and down.
> How the belfries rock and reel!
> How the great guns, peal on peal,
> Fling the joy from town to town!
>
> For the Lord
> On the whirlwind is abroad;
> In the earthquake he has spoken;
> He has smitten with his thunder
> The iron walls asunder,
> And the gates of brass are broken!
>
> Did we dare,
> In our agony of prayer,
> Ask for more than he has done?
> When was ever his right hand
> Over any time or land
> Stretched as now beneath the sun?

Here is no note of personal triumph, only reverential gratitude for the overruling hand. This is beautifully expressed in the Newburyport Hymn, the culminating poem of the war series.

> Not unto us who did but seek
> The word that burned within to speak,
> Not unto us this day belong
> The triumph and exultant song.
>
> The praise, O Lord, is Thine alone,
> In Thy own way the work is done.
> Our poor gifts at Thy feet we cast,
> To whom be glory, first and last.

The danger line was now passed. The transition from a harsh clime into an atmosphere of warmth and flowers was to be the felicitous fate of the abolitionists. Show me, in history, a parallel to this. In the beginning darkness over all the land, a system of iniquity seemingly impregnable. Slowly the light spreads, dangers and persecutions assail the forlorn hope, the siege through all vicissitudes is never raised, and at last the citadel falls. Marvelous future! The early soldiers lived to see a realization beyond their utmost dreams.

To be transformed from infidels and fanatics into champions of religious faith and conservators of truth was almost to lose identity. As the pioneer of abolition foresaw:

> Finally excessive panegyric is substituted for outrageous abuse. The praise, on the one hand, and the defamation on the other, are equally unmerited. In the clear light of Reason, it will be seen that he (the reformer) simply stood up to discharge a duty which he owed to his God, to his fellow men and to the land of his nativity."

The exit from the storm into calm waters finds sweet expression in the poem "My Birthday," a mingling of thankfulness with a suggested sense of loss for the past days of labor.

> How hushed the hiss of party hate,
> The clamor of the throng!
> How old, harsh voices of debate
> Flow into rythmic song!
>
> Methinks the spirit's temper grows
> Too soft in this still air;
> Somewhat the restful heart foregoes
> Of needed watch and prayer.
>
> The bark by tempest vainly tossed
> May founder in the calm,
> And he who braved the polar frost
> Faint by the isles of balm.

To read the personal poems of Whittier is to be ushered into a company of exalted spirits. One has but to name Follen, Channing,

Lucretia Mott

Daniel Neall, Joseph Sturge, Lydia Maria Child,[15] Lucretia Mott,[16] Garrison, Samuel E. Sewall, Sumner, George L. Stears, and other less remembered names, to realize the fellowship which devotion to a great cause brought in its line. When a tried comrade fell, it was the custom of the anti-slavery orators to pronounce the funeral tribute, and often for Whittier to embalm his memory in verse.

Value of Whittier's Reformatory Poems

I have of choice dwelt disproportionately on the influence of Whittier's reformatory poems, which, now that the special evils he fought have changed their shape, there is a disposition to undervalue. Those to whom the recollection of the long, desperate conflict is vivid, whose pulses were quickened by the poet's trumpet blasts, whose drooping faith was revived by his undaunted spirit, who, in the desert and the darkness were taught by him to

> Clothe the waste with dreams of grain,
> And, on midnight's sky of rain,
>   Paint the golden morrow,

only those can estimate aright the value of these paeans of liberty. How is it possible for conservative eyes to understand their depth or to comprehend the force of appeals to the moral sense and the ideal which the soul conceives? "It takes greatness to see greatness," said Theodore Parker, and surely it requires reformers to understand the utterances of reform.

The scholarly critics will record their verdicts: point out in proper phrase the defects and weigh the beauties of expression, and think with their polished rules to measure this man's greatness and fix his place in literature.

But unlettered men and women, to whom no college doors swung open, who confess an ignorance of literary art, and know only the rugged school of toil and sacrifice in the service of unpopular reform, will have a truer insight and better indicate the enduring quality of Whittier.

It would be interesting to know how much of the current worship of Whittier is sincere and appreciative, so conventional and popular has the celebration become. In the days when he was writing his indignant and fiery verses of protest and rebuke, it was the fashion to burn incense to the Revolutionary fathers. Men who justified chattel slavery were eloquent in laudation of John Hancock and Sam Adams, proudly quoting the language of James Otis and Patrick Henry, spoken in the days that tried men's souls.

It was lip-service and a hollow mockery. Not from the heart came these formal tributes to past greatness. To declaim the sentiments of the Declaration of Independence and then to justify the return of fugitive slaves was a stultification of morals, seemingly unperceived by the offenders.

Lydia Maria Child

Whittier societies and the preservation of relics is the imitation of his unconquerable defiance of popular wrong at the expense of reputation and applause. So only shall we be worthy to rejoice in his great memory.

The true test of reverence for past reformers is the attitude of the worshipper regarding national transgressions of their own day. Men who extol Whittier's virtues and courage while silent when the nation that gave liberty to four million slaves at home now holds in subjection eight million of human beings in the Orient, are fatally lacking in sensibility and understanding.

How much we need the lyrical inspiration matching that of Whittier and Lowell. But where can the great tones which they sounded be heard in contemporary verse? Professor Norton truly says:

> In poetry there is not a single commanding voice. Now and then a transient note of power is heard, but the strongest are those which deal with and for the most part glorify material things. The great harpers of the House of Fame have departed.

The praise of past times and heroes can wait until the equally heroic struggle for liberty now in progress can show deeds of similar valor and sacrifice. Better than

*"Garrison the Liberator"
statue in Brown Square
honors the
speaker's father,
William Lloyd Garrison*[17]

55

SALEM/DANVERS

Two commemorations honoring Whittier, the Quaker poet of Essex County, were held in neighboring Salem. The first was observed at the Essex Institute, now called the Peabody Essex Museum, with a large gathering of members and friends.

Alden P. White, Vice-President of the Danvers Historical Society, presided over the event. He noted the celebrations that were being observed particularly at the birthplace and in Amesbury, the latter having the most distinctive address by Booker T. Washington. He added that the institute was privileged to be presenting something original through the ladies of Oak Knoll.

White read a paper written by Mrs. Abbie J. Woodman, the poet's niece, describing Whittier's home life at Oak Knoll in Danvers. She reminisced about conversations, the literary visitors, the delights of the seasons, and his extensive correspondence.[18]

> He rested there safe from the jeers of the world, his fame achieved. His life
> there was ideal and in accordance with his tastes, for no more beautiful com-
> fortable place exists along the North Shore than that home of his.

Keep this circular in the Whittier collection copy of this book.

SALEM
APR 2
19 08
MASS.

Public Library
Bradfo...

REMINISCENCES OF JOHN GREENLEAF WHITTIER'S LIFE AT OAK KNOLL, DANVERS, by his cousin, Mrs. Abby J. Woodman, read before the Essex Institute on the one hundredth anniversary of his birth. The volume also contains a list of the first editions, portraits, engravings, manuscripts, and personal relics of John Greenleaf Whittier, exhibited at the Essex Institute, December 17, 1907 to January 31, 1908. The frontispiece is an engraved portrait after a photograph made in 1885.

8vo. 52 pages, full blue paper boards with paper label. 200 copies printed.

Price, $1.00, net, postpaid.

Address, THE ESSEX INSTITUTE,

Salem, Mass.

Inside page of Woodman's reminiscences and the envelope with note giving the book to the library

Oak Knoll

The Danvers cousins had expected Whittier to return to Oak Knoll after a trip to Hampton in September, 1892 but he died while away.

The secretary of the institute, George Dow, called special attention to the collection of souvenirs of the poet being exhibited at the institute. They were proud knowing that of the many works on exhibit, 179 were purely from first editions. In fact, theirs was the largest collection of first editions of Whittier ever brought together, and all but eleven were owned by the Essex Institute.

Other items included pictures, manuscripts, letters, souvenirs, the Quaker certificate of marriage of Whittier's parents, and a cane Whittier used. The exhibit was held in six cases. The newspaper article closed with a reference to another literary Centennial:

> When the Hawthorne centenary was celebrated, the Essex Institute was able to show in its collection a copy of every first edition of his works with a single exception, a collection not equaled elsewhere, and its Whittier collection in this line has no equal.

The second Whittier celebration in Salem was observed by The Thayer Club of the Crombie Street Church. Franklin B. Sanborn of Concord, well-known throughout New England as one of the surviving abolitionists, was the featured speaker.

Centenary Observed in Danvers

Newspaper accounts told of "one hundred of the best and most literary people of Danvers" who gathered at the new headquarters of the Historical Society[19] to commemorate the 100th birthday of Whittier. A large painting of Whittier was decorated by a wreath of holly and a vase of American Beauty roses was placed beneath the portrait. President Hines officiated and the Honorable A. P. White read Mrs. Abbie J. Woodman's paper on Whittier's life at Oak Knoll. Apparently, those who heard the reading in Salem said "it was much better in Danvers," and added that this was proof that the more it is studied and read, interest in it mounts.

Mrs. Sarah Richardson read "The Sycamores," "The Witch of Wenham Lake," and "Eternal Goodness."

The Page House, home of the Danvers Historical Society

Local paper highlights the commemoration

Franklin B. Sanborn

Franklin Benjamin Sanborn, at seventy-six, was a survivor of the turbulent years of the pre–Civil War Abolitionist movement. His colorful and passionate life (1831–1917) spanned decades of great change in all realms of life.

Born in Hampton Falls, NH, he followed political issues from boyhood, announcing even at age nine that he was against slavery.[20] He was a member of the "Secret Six" funding John Brown's activities.

As a journalist, social reformer, and Transcendentalist, he was closely associated with Emerson, Thoreau, and others of the Concord group, who, Sanborn pointed out, took up the cause of freedom after Whittier. Sanborn wrote biographies of many of them. He gave his first speech in Haverhill, then later at the Salem commemoration.[21] Sanborn gave a deeper perspective on Whittier's role in national politics than other speakers, and particularly addressed why ex-Presidents Washington, Adams, and Jefferson had not abolished slavery.

SANBORN'S ADDRESS

=================================

Whittier as Man, Poet, Reformer

It is no light task, in a brief space, to deal with the long and active life of one who was not only Man and Poet, and a Reformer in many directions, at the period of all others in our history abounding in the need and the diversity of reforms, political, religious, and social; but also a typical and representative New England citizen,—that character almost new in the world's long story, and destined to play so great a part in the drama of civilization on this continent.

John Greenleaf Whittier bore in both his family names the evidence that his ancestors had been among the early settlers of New England; and if it be true that he was also descended from a daughter of Christopher Hussey, then he was likewise of the posterity of that sturdy old colonizer Rev. Stephen Bachiler, born four years earlier than Shakespeare, and dying at nearly a hundred years old, in the denomination of his associate in religion, Oliver Cromwell, and his son Richard.

This clergyman, dispossessed of his parish in western England, at the suggestion of Bishop Laud, wandered for a time about England and Holland, and after doing his part to establish a religious colony at Portland in Maine, and Yarmouth in the Pilgrim Colony, did found and partly organize the ancient town of Hampton in New Hampshire, to which his son-in-law Christopher Hussey, and his three grandsons of the Sanborn name, followed him in 1638 or soon after.

The house in Hampton Falls, New Hampshire, in which Whittier died stands on a part of the large estate of Christo-pherHussey, and the house occupied by that patriarch of New Hampshire was not far off. Hussey also owned land in Haverhill, although he is not supposed to have lived there for any long time. In 1653, Thomas Whittier, the poet's paternal ancestor, joined with Hussey, Edward Gove, and the three Sanborn brothers in petitioning the Boston magistracy in favor of Major Pike of Salisbury, who had spoken too freely against the Boston tyranny in suppressing Joseph Peasley, another ancestor of Whittier, who felt a call to exhort in meeting, and afterward became a Quaker.

Hussey was then dwelling at Hampton Falls, and was one of the few petitioners who refused to withdraw their signatures, when bidden so to do by the Boston authorities; as Thomas Whittier and two of my ancestors, John Sanborn and Edward Gove, also refused, and were fined for their contumacy.

Influence of Quakerism

In the next generation most of the Husseys, Goves, and Whittiers were Quakers; for by 1675 George Fox had visited New England, the Boston and Dover Puritans had whipped and hanged Quaker women, — the graceless physicians Dr. Barefoot and Dr. Greenland, aided by Major Pike, now a high magistrate, had rescued the whipped women from the scourge of Major Waldron, — and the natural result of fervent preaching and bloody persecution had taken place.

Thus was Quakerism, itself a demonstration for radical reforms in church and state, handed down through the seventeenth and eighteenth centuries to our Poet, born in the first decade of the nineteenth century, and living in literary activity almost to the twentieth, for he died late in 1892.

Nor did this descendant of the martyred Quakers fail to remember their persecutions, and to visit poetic justice upon the persecutors and their successors in the business of bigotry and tyranny, — the intolerant sectarians and natural Tories of New England. The Quakers, all through the latter part of the eighteenth century and the first half of the nineteenth, had combined good citizenship and scrupulous obedience to decent laws, with a firm and demonstrative refusal to sanction negro slavery. But the so-called conservative classes — the clergy, the leading lawyers, the great merchants, and the politicians generally (with few exceptions after 1820, and until 1850) — were defenders or apologists for that blot on our Republic of Liberty.

Consequently, the Man, Whittier, imbued with the ancestral spirit of opposition to legalized tyranny, and fully possessed of the democracy of religion (which Quakerism is), first drew public attention as one of the antislavery convention at Philadelphia in 1833, at the age of twenty-five. He was already known as a poet in his small circle, and indeed had then written more verses in number, and more pages in what passed for poetry, than Gray or Emerson wrote during their whole lives.

But the general public hardly took note of these verses, which were eagerly read by his young contemporaries, and widely copied from the newspapers of his friends Garrison and Thayer, or from his own political newspapers, at Boston and Hartford. In these newspapers he advocated a protective tariff (as Garrison had done for a time) and the election of Henry Clay as President.

Whittier's Literary and Ethical Apprenticeship

His politics rather than his poetry interested the active men of his youth; but the question of slavery, which was to supersede all others in our politics, had not, till after 1830, taken a strong hold on the people of the North. But even as his youthful verses, now forgotten, served him as exercises in poetic composition, and his journalism trained him to be, as he afterward showed himself, a sagacious and adroit politician; so the years of his literary and ethical apprenticeship, from 1826 to 1833, slowly and almost unconsciously prepared him for the devotion of all the rest of his life to the great measures of reform, whether in his own land or elsewhere.

His father, the Quaker farmer of the East Parish, was a Jeffersonian democrat, like Clay, Calhoun, and in his own independent way, John Quincy Adams; and though the young journalist joined for a time the party of which Clay was the leader, and which called itself "Whig," he in fact adhered rather strictly to the Jeffersonian principles.[22]

An evidence of this is in his striking poem on "Democracy," written in 1841, and making allusion to his father's political affiliations. I quote from the earlier form of these verses, which seems better than the revision which the fastidious author made many years later. It began:—

O fairest born of love and light,
 Yet bending brow and eye severe

On all that harms the holy sight,
 Or wounds the pure and perfect ear!
Beautiful yet thy temples rise,
 Though there profaning gifts are thrown;
And fires, unkindled of the skies,
 Are glaring round thy altar-stone.

O ideal of my boyhood's time!
 The faith in which my father stood,
Even when the sons of Lust and Crime
 Had stained thy peaceful courts with blood.
Beneath thy broad impartial eye
 How fade the lines of caste and birth!
How equal in their suffering lie
 The groaning multitudes of earth!

Henry Clay

Out of these principles, from which the Quaker poet never departed, was developed, by a strange metamorphosis, the actual Democratic party of Whittier's early manhood under Jackson; against which the youthful politician revolted, at first under the lead of Henry Clay, himself nominally a Democrat.

Garrison, too, as a beginner in politics, followed the lead of Clay.... [23]

Up Against Conventional Christianity

Whittier... from the first was brought up as a Christian, though in much disregard of that form of conventional Christianity which attached importance to the office of the parish priest or minister. Nor was he, at first, very much addicted to the conventional religious literature, even of his own small sect.

It was the age of Scott, Moore, and Byron, following the age of Robert Burns, who seems to have been Whittier's first favorite among poets. From none of these popular poets could he have imbibed much reverence for the titled clergy; while from the history and traditions of his own people, he was sure to regard them as spiritual tyrants and bloody persecutors. Hence, in one of his first sallies against the Massachusetts clerisy, he recurred to the Puritan ministers who so violently tiraded against his ancestors, the Peasleys and Husseys. In his scathing rebuke of the Congregational clergy in 1837 he cried, sarcastically: —

Oh, glorious days! when Church and State
    Were wedded by your spiritual fathers;
And on submissive shoulders sate
    Your Wilsons and your Cotton Mathers!
No vile "itinerant" then could mar
    The beauty of your tranquil Zion,
But at his peril, — of the scar
    Of hangman's whip and branding iron.
Old Hampton, had her fields a tongue, —
    And Salem's streets, — could tell their story
Of fainting women dragged along;
    Gashed by the whip accursed and gory.

Whittier had learned thoroughly that dismal tale of the three Quaker women, Anna Coleman, Mary Tomkins, and Alice Ambrose, whom the old tyrant of Dover, Richard Waldron, had in 1662 ordered to be flogged at the cart's tail from the Pascataqua River to Narragansett Bay, but who were released by the bold Major Pike of Salisbury, at the instance of Walter Barefoot, of Dover, and Henry Greenland, then of Newbury. These two doctors would have been excellent subjects for a second of those quiet novels of which "Margaret Smith's Journal" was the first. Only their adventures would have been more boisterous than those of the gentle Margaret and her cousin Rebecca Rawson.

Poet of the Minority

Whittier was both poet and historian, as Scott was; and, had he not made himself quite early the poet of the Minority, he might have risen to more distinction as historical poet. As it is, he has contributed more to the ballad lore of New England than all the other poets; and this part of his work will perhaps outlast that which at first he regarded as more important, — his antislavery and reformatory verse.

In the latter he seemed to present a singular contrast between his Quaker and non-resistant principles and his belligerent words. This contrast attracted the laughing notice of Lowell, in his "Fable for Critics," who made his spokesman, Apollo, cry out: —

"Is that," one exclaims on beholding his
    knocks,
"Thy son's bloody garment, O leather-clad
    Fox?"
Can that be thy son, in the battle's mid din,
Preaching brotherly love, — and then driving
    it in
To the brain of the tough old Goliath of Sin
  With the smoothest of pebbles from
    Castaly's Spring,
Impressed on his hard moral sense with a
    sling?

Whittier was pleased at this recognition of the fighter under the drab coat; and I have seen a letter of his to Lowell complimenting the almost anonymous poet on his success in the "Fable."

To be a poet of the Minority is not always to be on the right side; but the greatest poets in the world have held that position. If we could know all the facts about the men who wrote the epics ascribed to Homer, it would probably be true of them; and certainly it was true of Aeschylus and Sophocles among the Greek dramatists; of Lucretius in Rome; Dante in Florence; Milton in England; Burns in Scotland; Wordsworth, Shelley, and Keats in England; and in our day it has been true of Browning there, and Emerson here.

This may be said, however, of the better poets of the Minority, — that if they represent, as they usually do, the higher national aspiration, the day comes, even in their lifetime, when the majority rally to their side, and they are for a while, at least, the voice of their nation. Dante never reached that fortunate day, but Milton did, and Wordsworth more slowly attained that position.

So, in this country, the poets of democracy and antislavery; and the popularity, which from the first attended the fortunate Longfellow overtook Bryant and Lowell and Whittier in the national crisis of the Civil War.

Mobs Attack Abolitionists

It does a poet of the right sort no harm to be mobbed a few times. Whittier was mobbed repeatedly in his early career; and twice was the serene Emerson mobbed, — at Cambridge in 1851, and at the Tremont Temple of Boston in the winter of 1860-61. In neither case was his life in danger.

But when Whittier and George Thompson were mobbed, it was a question of serious bodily harm, even of death, at the hands of the furious ruffians who were impelled by those persistent American anarchists, the men of large wealth and commercial greed, who know that their riches have been immorally gained. Such were the slave-masters and their mercantile friends at the North, who sought Garrison's life in 1835, killed Lovejoy in 1837, burned the antislavery hall at Philadelphia in May, 1838, and for more than twenty years longer continued to display their sneaking form of anarchy in all the chief cities of the North.

The last of this may have been the draft riots in Boston and New York in 1863; but by that time, and for a year or two before, the mob spirit turned against the defenders of slavery, and more than once compelled them to hang out the flag of their country, the Stars and Stripes; which, from the disgrace of protecting slave-auctions and floating over conquests made to extend negro slavery (as in the Mexican War), had suddenly, in 1861, become the flag of freedom once more.

Through all this dismal period of national infamy, Whittier and the small band of emancipationists stood firmly for the rights of man, the cause of the poor. But I hardly think Whittier was involved in any dangerous mob after 1845; he withdrew from the physical activity in the cause which he had displayed for a dozen years after 1832, left Haverhill for the quiet retirement of Amesbury and did his work, either with the pen, in prose and verse, or through his rare sagacity, by advice to political associates, or those whom he wished to make such.

65

Editing in Lowell

He had undertaken to edit newspapers at Hartford, at Philadelphia, and finally at Lowell, where in 1844 he took charge of a journal devoted to political antislavery, the *Middlesex Standard*, and wrote for it not only political articles, but those brief papers, descriptive of periods or characters in New England story, which he published long ago under the title of "The Stranger in Lowell."

In his capacity as editor in Lowell he became closely acquainted with the circle of young women who set going, and maintained for years, that interesting organ of literature among the factory girls,—the *Lowell Offering*. He knew Harriet Farley (who has lately died in New York at the age of ninety-two); her associate Harriet Curtis; a third Harriet, Miss Hanson, afterwards Mrs. W. S. Robinson of Concord and Malden; and Lucy Larcom, who continued to be an intimate friend so long as Whittier lived.

He was therefore a well-informed witness to that cultivation of literature among the native American factory girls of New England which was so surprising a feature of our development two generations ago.

It was during Whittier's summer at your neighboring "Spindle City" of Lowell that his friend Emerson was induced by the antislavery women of Concord to place himself squarely on the emancipation side, by his address on the anniversary of West India Emancipation, given in Concord, August 1, 1844.

Emerson Takes a Stand

My impression is that Whittier himself came over to report the proceedings of the day, and complained that Concord was a very mossgrown, stagnant sort of place; but that he found comfort in Emerson's Address, which took strong and new ground against the enslavement of a race by advantage of its virtues.

It was a day long to be remembered in Concord. Hawthorne had been for two years living in the Old Manse, and was publishing those "Mosses" which preserve that ancient parsonage in immortal youth. Not sympathizing himself very much with the emancipationists, he yet made no objection to Mrs. Hawthorne's offering to have the "collation" tables spread under the trees of his avenue, which was to have been the resort of the audience after the address was over. But the summer day was lowering or

Lowell Mills

66

Ralph Waldo Emerson

rainy, and the tables were set, instead, in the county court-house, near the antique stone prison of Middlesex.

To call the company together at the hour announced for the meeting, a bell must be rung; and the authorities of the two chief churches in the village, the Unitarian and Orthodox Congregational, were unwilling to have their bells rung on such an occasion. A bell was found, however, which did not refuse to ring when Henry Thoreau pulled the rope; and thus the faithful were summoned to the first of Emerson's strictly political addresses.

I owe a knowledge of these facts to a lively letter by Miss Anne Whiting in the *Herald of Freedom*, at Concord, New Hampshire, a weekly edited by Thoreau and Whittier's friend Nathaniel P. Rogers. No considerable part of the address appeared in Whittier's Lowell newspaper, the orator reserving it for a pamphlet edition, which he soon issued.

Looking for a Candidate for Congress

It was not long after this, and while Whittier had charge of the Lowell newspaper, that he offered to the poet Longfellow to have him nominated for Congress in the Middlesex District, on the Liberty Party ticket. A vacancy existed in this district, which then included Cambridge, Concord, and Lowell, because neither the Democratic nor the Whig party had been able to elect their candidate, on account of the considerable antislavery vote in the county.

Whittier had seen that the few antislavery poems of Longfellow, reprinted as a tract at the North, had been very well received, and he said to Longfellow that they "had been of important service to the Liberty movement." He therefore urged on his brother-poet the acceptance of a congressional nomination, saying "Our friends think they could throw for thee one thousand more votes than for any other man."

Dating his reply, September, 1844, Longfellow answered: —

It is impossible for me to accept the Congressional nomination you propose, because I do not feel myself qualified for the duties of such an office, and because I do not belong to the Liberty Party. Though a strong anti-slavery man, I am not a member of any society, and fight under no single banner.

At all times I shall rejoice in the progress of true liberty, and in freedom from slavery of all kinds; but I cannot for a moment think of entering the political arena. Partisan warfare becomes too violent, too vindictive for my taste.

This was not meant as a reproof to Whittier, but it indicated what was then a common view among educated men.

Sumner himself was then averse to politics, like his intimate friend Longfellow, and "could not for a moment think of entering the political arena." He also declined a congressional nomination, two years later, against Robert C. Winthrop, and allowed his intimate friend Dr. Howe to lose credit and influence by standing for Congress in his place. A few years later Sumner was forced to become a politician, upon his election to the Senate.

Indeed, Longfellow's brother-professor in Harvard College, Dr. Palfry, was nominated and chosen to Congress from this same Middlesex district; and it was in support of his reelection that Emerson made the speech in 1851 which procured for him a storm of hisses at the Cambridge public meeting.

Whittier never had scruples of this scholarly kind against engaging in politics. In early years of activity he had desired a

Henry Wadsworth Longfellow

nomination to Congress; he had been chosen to the State Legislature, had served there, and was ready at all times to take his part, with his fellow citizens, in the duties and discomforts of self-government. Nothing was farther from his thoughts than anarchy; he was one of the multitude himself, and depended on seeing the function of government duly performed in his province, whatever that province might be. If he thought ill of his country's Constitution, he knew how it could be improved, and he set to work to make things better.

He was never a believer in the non-voting hypothesis of government, and he separated from Garrison and the extreme abolitionists on that issue, among others. Like most of the Quakers, however, he did not believe in war; and made the mistake of supposing, as late as 1859, that slavery could be peacefully abolished.

"Political Prudence" of John Quincy Adams

Things had got beyond that even in 1847, when Whittier became one of the chief editorial writers for Dr. Bailey's *National Era*, the antislavery weekly established in Washington, after the cause of Liberty began to have bold defenders in the House and Senate at the national capitol. One of the first of these, in point of time, was the aged Ex-president John Quincy Adams, whose great political prudence had kept him from acting against slavery while president, and candidate for the presidency; but who, as early as 1820, had seen, with his native sagacity, that slavery and the Union could not continue long to coexist, and had entered in his Diary for February 24, in that year, this remarkable passage: —

I had some conversation with Calhoun on the slave-question pending in Congress. He said he did not think it would produce a dissolution of the Union; but if it should, the South would be compelled to form an alliance, offensive and defensive, with Great Britain. I said, that would be returning to the Colonial state. He said, "Yes, pretty much; but it would be forced upon them." I pressed the conversation no further.

But if the dissolution of the Union should result from the slave question, it is as obvious as anything that can be foreseen of the future, that it must shortly afterwards be followed by the universal emancipation of the slaves. Slavery is the great and foul stain upon the North American Union, and it is a contemplation worthy of the most exalted soul, whether its total abolition is or is not practicable; if practicable, by what means it may be effected, and if a choice of means be within scope, what means would accomplish it at the smallest cost of human suffering?"

Having thus stated the problem Mr. Adams went on to foretell its solution, in these extraordinary words, which our age has seen literally fulfilled, forty-odd years after they were inscribed in the secret diary of a secretary of state at Washington: —

A dissolution, at least temporary, of the Union as now constituted, would be necessary; and the dissolution must be upon a point involving the question of slavery and no other. The Union might then be reorganized on the fundamental principle of Emancipation. This object is vast in its compass, awful in its prospects, — sublime and beautiful in its issue. A life devoted to it would be nobly spent, — or sacrificed.

Many lives were, in effect, so sacrificed, but not Adams's own. He continued to uphold the Union as it was, — the Union fatally tied to the perishable barbarism of slavery, and certain, if the tie were not cut, to destroy both the country and its barbarism.

Whittier for many years, after opposing slavery with all his might, still cherished the delusion that it could be peacefully abolished. Once it could have been, had Washington and Jefferson, in the closing decade of the eighteenth century, followed the lead of Franklin, wisest man of his century, who pressed actively for emancipation, as did the real leaders of the French Revolution, and the English liberals. Both those great Virginians knew that Franklin was right; both were abolitionists; and Jefferson, who succeeded Franklin at the disorganized Court of the French monarchy, printed in Paris, in

Whittier is center photograph in poster "Champions of Freedom" — 1858

1785, those words of truthful description which have been so often quoted: —

> The whole commerce between master and slave is a perpetual exercise of the most boisterous passions, the most unremitting despotism, on the one part, — and degrading submissions on the other. With what execration should that statesman be loaded who, permitting one-half the citizens to trample on the rights of the other half, transforms those into despots and these into enemies, — destroying the morals of the one part and the patriotism of the other! And can the liberties of a nation be deemed secure when we have removed their only firm basis, — a conviction that these liberties are the gift of God, — that they are not to be violated without His wrath? I tremble for Virginia when I reflect that God is just; that His justice cannot sleep forever; that, considering numbers, Nature, and natural means only, a revolution of the wheel of Fortune is among possible events; that it may become probable by supernatural interference. The Almighty has no attribute than can take sides with us in such a contest.

Why, then, did not Washington and Jefferson, with their high-toned neighbor Colonel George Mason, act upon the considerations so forcibly stated? Because, I fancy, the political problems of their time were so pressing that they felt it a duty to hold the nation together, against the soured enmity of England, long coveting her revolted Colonies, and the wild ambition of Napoleon, which fluctuated between establishing an American empire based on negro slavery, and giving up the French possessions in America to strengthen our Republic against England, which was his real motive in selling Louisiana to Jefferson.

And our nation was held together, in spite of the angry disunion sentiment of the New England Federalists in 1804, ready to join with Aaron Burr in overthrowing the "Virginia dynasty," — and against the tendency to separation on the part of the Mississippi Valley States, a few years later; when Burr hoped, by their aid, to establish for himself a vast slaveholding empire in Louisiana, Texas, and Mexico. Thwarted in this by the sagacity of Jefferson and the honesty of Andrew Jackson, Burr betook himself to Europe, and there for years sought to betray his country either to England or to Napoleon, as either should offer him the highest personal bribe.

I have seen a letter from Washington by a New Hampshire member of Congress, John Adams Harper, in 1813, to his party leader, the Democratic Governor of New Hampshire, William Plumer, in which he reported an offer made by Napoleon, then beginning to be in straits after his failure in Russia, that he would join with England in dividing the troublesome American States at the Potomac, — Great Britain to take New England and the Northern half; and France, Virginia, Louisiana, and the Southern half.

This offer, if ever made, may have been only one of those schemes chasing each other through the restless mind of the French despot; but it would not have been unacceptable to some of the New England Federalists, who were quite ready, from 1812 to the victory of Jackson at New Orleans, to welcome an alliance with England, if not absolute dependence on the still reigning George III.

However this may be, the necessity of holding our young Republic together forbade efforts to abolish slavery by peaceful compensation; and by 1830 it had so

70

strengthened itself, with the aid of King Cotton, that the South became insolent, and refused even to consider its abolition. From that time forward, its destruction by force was the only solution of the problem, unless the North should be willing to see slavery made national, instead of decreasingly sectional.

For this bad purpose the annexation of Texas was carried; and the Mexican War was waged; and after 1848 the question, as a practical one, was no longer emancipation, but how to stop slavery extension and the reopening of the slave-trade. Upon that basis the Liberty party, of which Whittier was one of the chief founders, was merged in the Free-soil party of 1848, supporting Van Buren for the presidency against the Southern Whig General Taylor, and soon carrying Massachusetts by an alliance with the Jeffersonian democrats, headed by Boutwell and Rantoul.

Whittier Convinces Sumner

The disgust of Massachusetts at Webster's Fugitive-slave Law, and his seventh of March speech, in 1850, gave the election of that November into the hands of the coalition, and Whittier was then called upon to use his matchless powers of political combination and persuasion, to secure the election to the Senate of his friend Charles Sumner.

It was he who induced Sumner to be the candidate of the coalition, in the early winter of 1850–51; and, although at one point he advised Sumner to withdraw, in order to rebuke the bad faith of certain Democrats,—among them his old friend Caleb Cushing,—yet the candidate stayed in the field, and was elected, late in April, by a single vote. This was the beginning of Sum-

Charles Sumner

ner's great service to his native State, which continued till his death in 1874,—the most faithful servant and wisest statesman Massachusetts has had for a century.

When he was maliciously censured by a partisan legislature, for one of the best acts of his life, Whittier was unwearied in getting the stigma removed.

By this time the poet of the Minority had become the aged seer and adviser of the Majority; and well did Whittier perform this later duty. Good sense is not reckoned among the most conspicuous and expected qualities of poets; but it was characteristic of our Merrimac Valley poet from the first.

Had his health after childhood been as robust and cheerful as his common sense, he would have been a noted leader in the most active path of politics and reforms. But an early injury, growing out of his excessive farm-labors, kept him on the borders of invalidism all the rest of his days,

Illustration in "Snow-Bound" by Harry Fenn

and made him much more retired in his way of life than his natural tendency would have suggested.

He had the good Yankee quality of "sociability"; he was neighborly and even gossiping in his nature, and spent many hours in his village existence, sitting on stools and boxes in groceries and shoeshops, chatting with his townsmen. He did not put the company to flight, and check conversation, when he set foot in the familiar group seated around the stove, as Emerson complains that he did.

Nor was there ever a poet who better understood the conditions and sentiments of labor in New England; and his "Songs of Labor," in their merits and defects, went very close to the mark. He had been a laborer himself, and from first to last he sympathized with the upright industry and thrift of New England.

His familiarity with all that went to compose the idyll of rural life in New England,—the toil, the prayer, the nooning of Summer, the snow-bound days of Winter, the grace of Spring, the painted pageants of October,—the domestic life of women, the fun and earnest of the village,—the days of haymaking on the Salisbury and Hampton meadows, the freighting of hay on the Merrimac,—all this and more constitutes Whittier the laureate of ancient Essex and Rockingham, the two counties with which his early life made him best acquainted.

Few of us now survive who remember, of our own observation, all that he relates; but there it is, packed away, like honey in the hive, in the fascinating story of "Snow-Bound." It sounds a little strained to apply the word "great" to any one of Whittier's poems; but this one comes so near being a great poem, that the author's modesty must allow the designation.

The characters in "Snow-bound" stand out clear and fresh, like the persons in Homer; or, more exactly, they recall the rustic scenes and personages of Hesiod. This field of poesy—what has been called both pastoral and idyllic—belongs to Whittier by natural right, as much as his hexameters to Hesiod, or the Doric and Sicilian strains of Theocritus or Moschus.

Affectation is lacking; the picture is drawn, the person is presented, with all the offhand readiness of Nature herself. Only those who have forgotten the homely dialect of Rockingham and Essex will catch at some of Whittier's words as odd. They come naturally from him; and so do the colloquial misfits of accent and rhyme, that sometimes make the scholar smile.

Whittier would accent "romance" and "ideal" on their first syllable, and we let it pass; as in that favorite poem of his own "The Reformer," which to me, also, has ever seemed one of his best, both in thought and melody: —

> Young Romance raised his dreamy eyes
> O'erhung with paly locks of gold, —
> "Why smite," he asked, in sad surprise,
> "The fair, the old?"

The picture is a good one; indeed, this poem is a series of pictures, in verse wellnigh faultless: —

> All grim and soiled, and brown with tan,
> I saw a Strong One, in his wrath,
> Smiting the godless shrines of man
> Along his path.

> The Church, beneath her trembling dome,
> Essayed in vain her ghostly charm:
> Wealth shook within his gilded home,
> With strange alarm.

> Fraud from his secret chambers fled
> Before the sunlight bursting in:
> Sloth drew her pillow o'er her head
> To drown the din.

> "Spare," Art implored, "yon holy pile!
> "That grand, old, time-worn turret spare!"
> Meek Reverence, kneeling in the aisle,
> Cried out "Forebear!"

> Gray-bearded Use, who, deaf and blind,
> Groped for his old accustomed stone,
> Leaned on his staff, and wept to find
> His seat o'erthrown.

All this shocks the poet; but after a pause he looks again: —

> The grain grew green on battle-plains,
> O'er swarded war-mounds grazed the cow;
> The slave stood forging from his chains
> The spade and plow.
>
> . . . . .
>
> Through prison walls, like Heaven-sent hope,
> Fresh breezes blew, and sunbeams strayed;
> And with the idle gallows-rope
> The young child played.
>
> . . . . .
>
> The outworn rite, the old abuse,
> The pious fraud transparent grown,
> The Good held captive in the use
> Of Wrong alone, —

> These wait their doom, —from that great law
> Which makes the past time serve To-day:
> And fresher life the world shall draw
> From their decay.

> O backward-looking son of Time!
> The new is old, the old is new;
> The cycle of a change sublime
> Still sweeping through.

Here is the optimism, and something of the mysticism, of Emerson and Thoreau; and this poem dates from 1846, when the summer of Transcendentalism was not yet waning into autumn. But this optimism was sometimes amiss in its confident prediction; as in that mistaken ballad of Whittier on "Brown of Osawatomie," which, late in 1859, hardly fifteen months before the outbreak of the Civil War, and while the murders in Kansas were scarcely ended, declared that the day of battle was over: —

Nevermore may yon Blue Ridges the North
    ern rifle hear
Nor see the light of blazing homes flash on
    the negro's spear!
But let the free-winged angel Truth their
    guarded passes scale,
To teach that Right is more than Might, a
    Justice more than mail.
So vainly shall Virginia set her battle in ar
    ray;
In vain her trampling squadrons knead the
    winter snow with clay.
She may strike the pouncing eagle, but she
    dares not harm the dove;
And every gate she bars to Hate shall open
    wide to Love!

John Brown

Whittier's mistake here was twofold; he assumed, contrary to the fact, that John Brown was inspired by hatred of the slaveholders; and he exaggerated the power of Christian love in dealing with men in a passion. The Virginians of 1859 were no longer capable of considering calmly the emancipation of their slaves, as they might have done while Washington and George Mason were living; they misinterpreted every effort to free the land from its worst clog and contradiction, negro slavery.

As for Brown, his hatred of the barbarism of slavery was complete; but he regarded all men with a broad charity, and preferred to believe them good men until their actions showed the contrary. Unlike as he was in externals to Coventry Patmore's gentle heroine, it could be said of him as of her: —

> His life, all honor, observed with awe,
> Which cross experience could not mar,
> The fiction of the Christian law,
> That all men honorable are.

This also was Whittier's turn of mind, after he had outgrown the vehemence of his

John Brown

early onslaughts against classes and persons; it is, indeed, the principle of the higher Quakerism.

Brown was wiser than Whittier, when he said on the last day of his Virginia prison-cell:

> I am now quite certain that the crimes of this guilty land will never be purged away but with blood. I had, as I now think, vainly, flattered myself that without very much bloodshed it might be done.

Six years had to pass, and the winter snow be five times trampled with the red clay of Virginia, before either Love or Hate could open the door to Richmond. Even then another martyr must be added to Brown, and the myriads who followed him in death; and Abraham Lincoln must die by an assassin, ere the cause for which Brown and Lincoln died could peacefully prevail. The bullet as well as the ballot was needful to destroy Slavery; and that

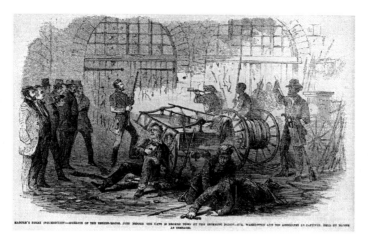

Harper's Ferry Insurrection
Hostages on left

our poet lived to see. Then, in fact, after years of battle, —

> Where frowned the fort, pavilions gay,
>   And cottage windows, flower-entwined,
> Looked out upon the peaceful ba
>   And hills behind,

and the aged bard could sing, as he had chanted forty years earlier, —

> Grown wiser for the lesson given,
>   I fear no longer; for I know
> That where the share is deepest driven,
>   The best fruits grow.

BOSTON

Boston's Whittier Centenary festivities began in the morning with special commemorations in every Boston public school from primary grades to the high schools. Such programs were similar and consisted of biographical sketches, singing of poems set to music, recitation, and addresses—all resounding the praise of the poet. It was reported that in most instances parents and friends could attend the programs.

At the Boston Latin School, five hundred boys listened to an address by Henry Pennypacker, one of the headmasters. Mr. Pennypacker's father and grandfather were closely associated with Whittier. He shared personal reminiscences that had been shared by his family. Newspapers noted that Dorchester's John Greenleaf Whittier School was the only school in Boston named after the poet. Boston's schools closed for the afternoon.

"Poet-Laureate of Freedom"

Newspaper accounts in Boston hailed Whittier as the "Poet Laureate of Freedom." Flags at all public buildings in the city were ordered "thrown to the wind." Newspapers reported that hundreds of people attended the "notable gatherings" held under the auspices "of the colored citizens."

The chairman of the two Centennial events in Boston was William Monroe Trotter, President of the New England Constitution and Suffrage League and a central figure in Boston's African-American community. Harvard-educated, the first man of color to be awarded a Phi Beta Kappa key and a successful businessman, Trotter was a political activist working to advance the lives of African-Americans.

He had co-founded *The Guardian* in Boston with George Forbes in 1901 in the same building that had housed William Lloyd Garrison's *The Liberator*. In his editorials, he took issue with Booker T. Washington's accommodation with white institutions. Only a few years earlier, he and Forbes had attended a speech in Boston given by Washington, and were arrested following a confrontation over his views on race.

William Monroe Trotter

As the events were being planned, Trotter placed an announcement of the Centennial in *The Guardian* lauding Whittier's commitment to abolition.

> …his poems today show agitation on the sin and shame of slavery. He treated the subject [of slavery] from almost every point of view and a reading of his poems today show[s] that he sought to reach and arouse the conscience of the northern whites against the monstrous system.

> He was almost as practical an agitator with poetry as Garrison was with prose. He can indeed be fittingly called the 'Poet Laureate of Abolition.' Nor was he less active for freedom as a man of affairs and as a practical politician.

> Surely it would be unbecoming for Colored Americans to allow the centenary of so great a friend of our rights and liberties go unnoticed. As chairman of the committee of the Suffrage League of Boston and vicinity, appointed to fitly celebrate this great day in Boston, I appeal to the Colored citizens in every city, town and hamlet in the land to heed the call of this league, supported by the New England Suffrage and Constitution league…to unite in a fitting celebration of the 100th anniversary of the sainted Whittier. Let the race-rights organizations who are contending for liberty as Whittier did take the lead and call the citizens at large to this duty.

> We can no better secure and keep friends of our liberties today than by honoring those who strove and suffered for our liberties in the days of chattel slavery. Will the press help by publishing this notice and urging their readers to this sacred duty.

FAITH IN COLORED RACE

This Is Col. T. W. Higginson's Message

Recalls the Fortitude of the Poet Whittier

His Growing Popularity in the South

Other Notable Speakers Eulogize Quaker Poet

Parker Memorial Hall was the site of the first of two Greater Boston citizens' celebrations on December 17, 1907. Children and people of all walks of life gathered in the afternoon to honor Whittier. Each Boston grammar and high school class was entitled to choose one delegate to attend the commemoration.

Colonel Thomas Wentworth Higginson was scheduled to be the main speaker for the afternoon's observance. He was a radical abolitionist, former Unitarian minister, and friend and biographer of Whittier.

As a younger man, Higginson had also distinguished himself in the military. He served as Commander and Colonel of the first African American regiment raised

Army portrait
Thomas Wentworth Higginson

in the service of the United States during the Civil War, recruiting runaway and freed slaves to fight against the Confederacy.

Thomas Wentworth Higginson
age 80

His infantry preceded the more famous Fifty-fourth Massachusetts Infantry, led by Robert Gould Shaw. Higginson later wrote about his wartime experience in *Army Life in a Black Regiment* (1870).

Higginson also mentored poet Emily Dickinson over a thirty-year period editing and eventually publishing (with Mabel Loomis Todd) a collection of her poetry.

As one of the eldest abolitionists of the nineteenth century, Higginson had turned down invitations to several Whittier commemorations, committing himself to the afternoon Boston event.

However, as the day arrived, Higginson, now 84 years of age, was not well enough to attend, nor give his address. In his stead, Benjamin Ferris delivered it.

There is no place where Whittier can be more justly or affectionately commemorated than in a convention of colored men and their friends.

The words of Whittier have now gone abroad more widely through the English-speaking world than those of any American but Longfellow; though they stop, unlike Longfellow's, before crossing the British channel to the European continent. In this country, I found them within a few years in southern bookstores, where they helped abolish slavery. Looking back at my own arrival there during the Civil War to enlist my black regiment, I find that I quoted in my own letter written home, at six o'clock on the very morning of my arrival, in 1862, gazing out on Hilton Head, a verse from Whittier and no one else:

> The tent-lights glitter in the land,
> The ship-lights on the sea;
> The night wind smooths with drift-
>   ing sand
> Our tracks on lone Tybee.

It sums up in memory the whole spirit of that delightful period—the happiest of a long life—when I was in command of a black regiment, the first one enlisted during our great Civil War, and when for nearly two years I lived in a tent and went to sleep without personal anxiety, knowing that there was a black sentinel at my tent door.

The faith I had during the war in the members of that colored race remains still unbroken. Those who did so well then can be trusted in time of peace, and they will hold out against oppression, whether the oppressors be depraved or only ignorant. Truth cannot prevail by mere loudness of voice and narrowness of temper on the part of its supporters. They must allow for differences of opinion among themselves, each doing his work in a manly fashion, and letting others do theirs in their own way. We must all remember that as this is Whittier's day, it is also the day of his friends, and they must recall his chant of the Negro boatmen at Port Royal with the moral he draws from it:

> We only know that God is just,
> And every wrong shall die.
> That laws of changeless justice bind
> Oppressor with oppressed;
> And, close as sin and suffering joined,
> We march to Fate abreast.

===============================

Other presentations spoke of Whittier's poetry as well as his work as an abolitionist. George G. Bradford and A. E. Pillsbury, prominent activists in Boston, were also unable to attend and sent letters to Chairman Trotter. Pillsbury wrote, in part:

> New England itself never produced, even in Benjamin Franklin, a more remarkable character than this Yankee Quaker, sage, saint, politician and poet.

In one of the most inspiring parts of the afternoon, three hundred public school children representing the city's elementary, grammar, and high schools sang some of the poems of Whittier that had been set to music.

Tributes and Warnings at Fanueuil Hall

At the Whittier Centenary commemoration that evening in Fanueuil Hall, the speakers' addresses were more political than in any other of the "Whittier-Land" locales. Chairman Trotter introduced the speakers, social activists Henry B. Blackwell and the Rev. Reverdy C. Ransom, who described conditions under which Negroes lived in the South comparing those in Jamaica, the latter locale being more progressive.

Blackwell, considered by Trotter as one of the "old war horses in the cause of suffrage," offered a personal tribute to Whittier in the struggles for freedom. At the same time, he decried the lack of progress in equality for his race. Receiving wild applause, he ended his speech with a warning whose message was still being heard more than fifty years later:

> And the day will come when free America will recognize the colored man and woman as the equal of the white man and woman.

With the audience cheering, he concluded with the following verse of Whittier:

> Our Fathers to their graves have gone,
> Their fight is fought, their battle won,
> But sterner trials wait the race
> Which rises in their honored place.
> A moral warfare with the crime
> And folly of an evil time;
> So let it be, in God's own might
> We gird us for the coming fight,
> And strong in him whose case is ours
> In couplet with unholy powers
> We grasp the weapons he has given,
> The light, the truth, and love of Heaven.

Riverdy C. Ransom — Orator of His Race

The audience gave a rousing ovation to Ransom, who was introduced as "the best known orator of his race." He was one of the leading A.M.E. clergymen, and years later was to become a bishop. Ransom proceeded to deliver a Centennial oration to Whittier and then, like Blackwell, quickly turned to attack the secretary of war, William H. Taft, and President Roosevelt. Civil rights activists and reformers would continue to say for the next century, he "appealed to the nation for the impartial enforcement of the Constitution, irrespective of color or creed."

Ransom concluded with:

> The next presidential election will be historical, because, for the first time the Negro will cast his vote, not because of what the Republican party said or did a generation ago, but because of what it is doing now. Those whose political property we have been may expect to find us in our accustomed place no longer.

Mrs. Agnes Adams, introduced as "an energetic worker for the uplifting of her own race," spoke of the impact of one of Whittier's poems, 'Tell Them We Are Rising.'" She noted, "This motto was adopted by the women of the race forty-three years ago. We know we have made mistakes on our road, but we are proud of our successes, and today in the words of Whittier, we can still say, "We are Rising."

WHITTIER EXHIBIT AT THE BOSTON PUBLIC LIBRARY

The Boston Public Library's Whittier Exhibit was impressive. It featured nearly all of his writings, beginning with the *Legends of New England* and the *History of Haverhill, 1823*, which although written by Whittier, was issued under the name B. L. Mirick. Scarce items included a piece of sheet music written in 1852 titled *Little Eva, Uncle Tom's Guardian Angel*, words written by Whittier.

Arranged in the fine arts department of the library, some forty-one first editions were featured in the exhibit. In addition, Houghton, Mifflin and Co., Whittier's publisher, loaned the library a collection of portraits of Whittier from 1830 until 1894, together with several of the original drawings for illustrated editions of Whittier's works. The drawings were by Burns, Mitchell, and other illustrators of a generation ago.

THE BROWNING CLUB

The Browning Club observed the Centennial at the Hotel Somerset with reminiscences of Whittier. Additional readings from Browning and Whittier made for interesting comparisons and contrasts.

Portraits of John Greenleaf Whittier: Ages 33, 43, 49, 73 and 80

OTHER TRIBUTES

New England was not the only locale where Whittier Centennial observances were held. New York; Washington; Chicago; Whittier, CA; and cities in Michigan and elsewhere also gave tribute to the life and works of John Greenleaf Whittier.

Municipal observances of this anniversary were certainly the largest gatherings. But private groups and organizations such as the American Missionary Association, the Alliance Chapter Junior Sons and Daughters of the Revolution, and literary groups also observed this day. While most of the newspapers reported the Centennial celebrations held during December of 1907, many local and national newspapers and magazines printed tributes and remembrances during 1908 as well.

In 1908, the Whittier Home Association celebrated another milestone: its first ten years. The members continued to raise funds for a Whittier statue through direct solicitation with letters to individuals, businesses, and many women's clubs around the world.

The following pages display examples of tributes in the form of invitations, magazine covers, excerpts from commentaries in magazines, as well as interesting miscellaneous clippings from the Whittier Home Association scrapbooks.

The Centennial celebration in Whittier, California took place at Whittier College and its program was similar to those in the east: letters presented, recitations, music and a major address. A portrait of Whittier was presented to the College. President Charles E. Tebbetts read letters written by Whittier years earlier to the town along with the poem he wrote to the town of Whittier when it adopted his name.

My Name I Give To Thee

Dear Town, for whom the flowers are born,
Stars shine, and happy songbirds sing,
What can my evening give to thy morn,
My Winter to Thy Spring? A life not void of pure intent
With small desert of praise or blame;
The Love I felt, the Good I meant,
I leave Thee with My Name.

The address was given by Rev. Alexander McGregor, a young minister in Amesbury from 1883 to 1885 and who had many talks with Whittier. He highlighted the influence the Scottish bard, Burns, had on the poet. At the close of his speech, Dr. McGregor suggested:

> every man in this city have the privilege of giving a dollar, every woman a half dollar and every boy and girl a dime and with these gifts of our people perpetuate in imperishable bronze or marble a statue to adorn our park. That in the future years the children and the people will say, ''That is our Whittier'. Wait not for some rich man or woman — let it be the expression of all people.

In 1987 during the celebration of the 100th anniversary of the founding of the community, the citizens of Whittier, California honored him with a statue by Tita Hupp commemorating "The Barefoot Boy" located near City Hall and another of the poet by Christoph Ritterhausen in Central Park.

HITTIER CENTENNIAL
AT WHITTIER CALIFORNIA

...ress Given By Former Amesbury Pastor--Movement to Erect Statue

...in receipt of a c...y of the ...Register of Dec. 18, published ...hittier, Los Angeles County, ...nia. This place was named ...e poet Whittier and naturally ...celebration of the 100th anniver- ...f the poet's birth. The issue of ...gister received gives an account ...e celebration held on Tuesday the ... It took place at the College and ...very largely attended. The Col- ...ge Glee Club rendered several of ...Whittier's poems. Pres. Tebbetts read ...etters which passed between Whittier ...and Hervey and Dr. Lindlay relating ...to the naming of the town and ...c llege. He also rea... the poem writ- ...ten to the town of Whittier by Mr. ...Whittier.

A reading from Snow Bound was given, followed by a paper on "The ...oet of the Home" by Mrs. A. D. Clark and a Historical Sketch of Whittier and the anti-slavery move- ...ment by Prof. Boston.

...The address of the evening was ...given by Rev. Alexander McGregor ...whose subject was "Whittier as I Knew Him." Mr. Gregor was a young ...inister in Amesbury from 1883 to ...1885 and often met Mr. Whittier and had many talks with him. In his ...address he related many interesting ...incidents of his talks with the p et, ...laying particular stress upon his love ...for Burns and the influence the Scot- ...tish bard had upon Whittier's life. In ...c osing his able address, he sug- ...gested that "every man in this city ...have the privilege of giving a dollar, ...very wom n a half dollar and every ...boy and girl a dim and with these ...gif s of our people per etuate in im- ...perishable bronze or marble a statue ...to adorn our park. That in the future ...y ars the children and the people will ...s y, "That is our Whittier Wait not ...for some rich man or woman—let it ...be the xpression of all the people."

Dr. McGregor asked all who would ...give the sums indicated and two-thirds ...f the audience a os .

On be alf of the Woman's Auxiliary, ...Mrs. A. C. Johnson presented the ...college with a large portrait of the ...Poet Whittier which was accept d by ...the president.

Dr. McGregor is well remembered ...by many of our people when he was ...pastor of the Methodist c urch which ...at that time st od on Pond street. His ...ministr here was very successful.

NO SALOONS, NO JAIL, NO POOR HOUSE AT WHITTIER

Wonderfully Active Town Near Los Angeles Named after Poet

A day in California which I shall remember with pleasure was that on which I took a short trolley ride from Los Angeles to the town of Whittier, named in honor of the Quaker poet. There are many mem- bers of the society of Friends in Cali- fornia and on that day a large meet- ing was held in the Friends meeting house, one of the best church edifices in the town. All speakers participated in the exercises, and the business sessions and all the services were of interest.

Whittier is only twenty years old, and already has a population of 4,000. It is fourteen miles from Los Angeles, with which it is connected by both steam and electric railways. Twenty electric cars each way run daily be- tween that town and Los Angeles. It is in a curve of the Puente foothill and from its elevat- ed position one can look down on the fertile San Gabriel Valley. It is in the frostless belt and flowers bloom all the year. The town has electric lights, gas and telephone service, as- phalt pavements are on business streets, and other public ways are graded, graveled and oiled. Side- walks, curbs and gutters are of cement. The town owns its own water works, and pure water comes from artesian wells six hundred feet deep.

As Whittier has no winter, vege- tables can be had from the gardens all the y ar where there is an oppor- tunity as in most cases, to irrigate . One daily and two weekly papers are published in the town. Thirty thous- and dollars has recently been appro- priated for a State Pathological Laboratory. A masonic temple has lately been built costing $15,000 and a new bank building on which $75,000. have been spent. Graded schools of a high order are enjoyed by Whittier pupils, high school building costing $80,000. Whittier college also stands well among similar institutions. Its corps of trained teachers coming from prominent American and English universities. that has an endowment of $150,000.

Whittier has a beautiful public library building on which $20,000 was expended one half of which was do- nated by Andrew Carnegie. No saloon disgraces the town and it has no jail or poor house. Fraternal orders to the number of nearly twenty, thrive in the Quaker town, and a hospital complete in all its appointments is there for the benefit of the ailing and unfortunate. Ten church edifices of pleasing architecture belong to as many different denominations.

Except during the rainy season in winter, the land in all this region must be irrigated to obtain crops. The orange takes the lead among the fruits. Lemons are also extensively grown, as are English walnuts. One thou and dollars worth of lemons have been grown on a single acre and $1,700 worth of oranges. Last year six hundred and fifty cars of oranges and two hundred and fifty cars of lemons were sent from Whittier. There are at present about 5,500 acres of walnut orchards in the vicinity of the Friends' settlement. Berries are also largely grown, the crop often netting $100 an acre.

California has its oil wells and from those near Whittier, employing eighty men, 96,000 barrels of oil per month are obtained.

P. P. Whitehouse.

CHICAGO CONGREGATIONAL CLUB

FORE FATHERS DAY FESTIVAL

287th Anniversary of the
Landing of the Pilgrims
Plymouth, Dec. 21st, 1620

134th Anniversary of the
Boston Tea Party
Boston, Dec. 16th, 1773

ONE HUNDREDTH ANNIVERSARY
OF THE BIRTH OF

John Greenleaf Whittier

HAVERHILL, MASS., DEC. 17, 1807

**Auditorium Hotel
Chicago**

CHICAGO CONGREGATIONAL CLUB
SI CUT PATRIBUS SIT DEUS NOBIS
CORPORATE SEAL
ORG. 1883. ∞∞ INC. 1907.

**Monday Evening
Dec. 16, 1907**

S. E. KNECHT
Secretary

JOHN J. MOORE
Treasurer

REV. WILLIAM E. BARTON, D.D., President

LADIES' NIGHT

Full page spread from The Washington Star newspaper

LADY WHO CAME ACROSS THE CONTINENT

Spent Three Days In Whittier Land and Took Home Many Souvenirs

Among the out of town guests who came down in the special car f om Boston Tuesday to the Whititer Centennial were two ladies who weremany miles from home. One had come across the whole width of the continent, her home being in Spokane, Washington, and her name, Mrs. Minnie Beard O'Neill. Her friend, Miss Frances Mills, came from Mt. Vernon, Iowa.

Mrs. O'Neill is a great lover of Whittier and very familiar with his poems. She spent three days in Whittier-land, starting for home Thursday afternoon and about the last thing she did was to secure a copy of the Whittier Centennial edition of the Daily News to take home with her. She visited all of the places made famous by Whittier; while at the birthplace she toasted apples in the big fireplace before which the poet had sat as a boy and eat a piece of pumpkin pie off from the ancient table used by Whittier family. She went to the babbling brook and secured pebbles from its bed to take home with her, visited the site of the old school house, se-cured a piece of bark from the elm tree made famous by "In School Days". She crossed the river to West Newbury, visiting the home of The Countess, securing a piece of clapboard from the Peasel-e house which had a hand-made nail in it, this she intended having made into a souvenir. All of the points of interest in this town were also visited. Thursday afternoon she spent an hour with Mr. Pickard at the Home, who showed her all of the valuable souvenirs of the poet.

She has a great infatuation for securing souvenirs of the poet and said she had at home a white collar that had been worn by Whittier. When she gets home she is going to make a Whittier corner in one of the rooms of the house. She has contributed to the statue fund and is a member of a Whittier club.

Her enthusiasm for the great poet is only an example of the high estimation in which the poet is held by people all over the world. She is not an Eastern lady but was born in Iowa and has always resided in the West.

THE BOOK NEWS MONTHLY

Vol. 26   *December, 1907*   *No. 4*

WHITTIER CENTENARY NUMBER

Whittier the Man

His Life *and* Personality

By Caroline Ticknor

Miss Ticknor is a member of the old New England family of Ticknors. She knows the Massachusetts that Whittier knew and loved. Her facts have been obtained from the Whittier family direct and are therefore to be relied upon.—THE EDITOR.

THE Old World may have her Goethe, her Schiller, and her Tennyson—but she has no Whittier," exclaimed Horace Staunton in 1870, and one may reiterate the saying 1907, concluding, "nor has the New World brought forth such another, although a century has rolled away since birth of this bard."

Now, at the century's close, the "Quaker Poet" serenely holds the place assigned him by Parkman, who said on the occasion of his seventieth birthday—"John Greenleaf Whittier, the poet of New England: his genius drew its nourishment from her soil; his pages are the mirror of her outward nature, and the strong utterance of her inward life."

Indeed, the relationship of the "Quaker Poet" to his New England, one so warm, so personal, is without parallel in the history of poets, except perhaps in the case of the "Rustic Bard." It is a curious fact that Whittier, the angelic, and Burns, the man of many faults and frailties, should have evoked in their readers and countrymen a kindred response. And Burns was Whittier's literary godfather. The falling into the boy's hands of a volume of his poems was the beginning of an epoch to the youth nurtured on dry treatises regarding Quakerism. In the Scotchman the lad discovered a great poet and a brother, and life was ever after a different thing to him.

Whittier's ancestry were sturdy farmerfolk, able-bodied, strong-minded, and his mother and father were the stuff of which heroes and martyrs are made, for the Quakers of that day had not forgotten the persecution of their fathers, and they stood ready to sacrifice everything on the altar of their faith.

John Greenleaf Whittier, the second of four children, was born in the house built by his paternal ancestor in the East Parish of Haverhill, Massachusetts, on December 17, 1807. He was a farmer's son, and as a boy he early did his share of the household chores, working with his father and uncle in the fields and forests. In later years he was accustomed to attribute his delicacy of health to the methods of toughening the constitution in vogue when he was a lad. Moreover, the drive to the Friends' Meeting at Amesbury, eight miles away, twice a week, with no buffalo robes or warm wraps, was thoroughly chilling, as was the interior of the meeting-house.

At fifteen years of age, Whittier had attained his full height, five feet ten and one-half inches; he is described as having a figure slender and straight as an Indian, a beautiful head with refined features, black eyes full of fire, dark complexion, a fine smile, and a lively but nervous man-

Whittier *as a* Combatant

In the Days *of the* Abolitionists

By Thomas Wentworth Higginson

One of the Few *Survivors of the* Group *to* Which Whittier Belonged

PROFESSOR LONGFEL-LOW wrote in his diary on December 4, 1857: "Met Whittier at the publishers. He grows milder and mellower, as does his poetry." This was just a fortnight before Whittier's fiftieth birthday.

Those who in later years saw him as a quiet and reticent elderly man among the circle of poets who seemed men of the world beside him, could hardly recognize him who had in his youth traveled through New England with George Thompson, the English abolitionist, and had been mobbed at every turn. Nor could they appreciate how resolutely he took the part of the voting abolitionists, whose children formed the Republican party of later years, and who were opposed to the non-voting or disunion abolitionists, headed by his early friend, Garrison. It is, therefore, worth while to show him in his more combative days —days whose lingering trace was visible in the pike, preserved in his modest study in old age, a weapon which had originally belonged to one of John Brown's men.

It is in memory of this combative quality that I now print a conversation with Whittier in his middle life, when he frankly described Garrison, as seen from his point of view, mentioning also a lady who was, perhaps, the most influential leader, through Garrison, of the anti-slavery movement. She was a person of singular power and charm, but one who carried all the bitter hostilities of that period into her few writings, and especially into her life of Harriet Martineau, whose ardent admirer she was. My talk with Whittier follows, as written at the time:

"On Saturday, September 21 [1849], I saw Whittier, and among other talk was mentioned [Elizur] Wright's attack on Garrison in the 'Chronotype,' which I

spoke severely of, but Whittier partially excused by saying that Wright had suffered so much from that clique [the disunion abolitionists] that he could not but feel strongly. 'It is essentially true what

John G. Whittier
After a bust by W. O. Partridge
Showing the poet in middle life

he says of Garrison,' said he, 'I know him thoroughly and know that he is a despot.'

"'But,' said I, 'you cannot justify Wright's assertion that Garrison cares for the slave only as a means for his own aggrandizement?'

"'No,' said he emphatically, 'far from it. But Garrison identifies the movement absolutely with himself. He is a Robespierre, with the same perfect self-consecration and the same absolute incapacity of tolerating those who differ from himself; his course has been from the beginning that of Robespierre, stopping short of bloodshed.'

"'It may be partially so,' said I, 'but he has been placed in a trying position. At the beginning he stood with remarkable prominence as undisputed sole head of

Whittier's Quakerism

By John Russell Hayes

Librarian *of* Swarthmore College

IKE dear Charles Lamb, half Quaker as he seemed—our Whittier loved Quaker ways and Quaker worship. He venerated the Quaker principles, finding in the silence of the First-day Meeting that true peace and quiet, that refuge from the noises and clamors of the multitude, that union of solitude and society, that possession of the spirit's depth in stillness, which were so grateful, so consoling, to "Elia."

If Charles Lamb, slipping away at times from the janglings and nonsense-noises of the world, to enjoy a quiet half-hour upon some undisputed corner of a bench among "the gentle Quakers," has drawn an immortal picture of the unworldly sect, how much more fully and constantly, though not more beautifully—for that

were impossible—has Whittier portrayed the very spirit and atmosphere of the Friends' devotions. His poems on the theme are redolent of the sunny peace of ancient country graveyards lying so wistfully, so silently, within their box-hedges or old stone walls; his verse is fragrant of the golden calm that prevails inside the dignified and venerable meeting-houses, those old-time homes of prayer, sanctified by the worship of generations of quiet men and women, the marriages and the burials of kindly and gracious souls through year on tranquil year. I know few literary and spiritual joys greater than the reading of Whittier's Quaker poems on a still First-day afternoon of summer among the graveyard flowers and evergreens, or beneath the meeting-house oaks on some soft October noon. The

The Whittier Pine
Above Squam Lake, in New Hampshire
A spot that Whittier loved

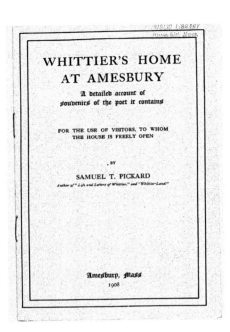

WHITTIER'S HOME AT AMESBURY

A detailed account of souvenirs of the poet it contains

FOR THE USE OF VISITORS, TO WHOM
THE HOUSE IS FREELY OPEN

· BY

SAMUEL T. PICKARD

Author of "Life and Letters of Whittier," and "Whittier-Land."

Amesbury, Mass
1908

ENDNOTES

1. Oil painting rendering signed "Sargent" [1960s]

2 Research by Frances Dowd, a past President of the Whittier Home Association.

3 In *A House Becomes A Home,* "Ben" Pickard writes:

> Lizzie, who worked with them in all their projects, had often indicated that she wanted the Association to continue the management of the house after her death, so the Association assumed that when the lease expired in 1903 they would either purchase the house, renew the lease, or better still, have the house given to them. A year or so before her death, however, Lizzie changed her mind and stipulated to her husband that she wanted the house left to her son Greenleaf, provided he wanted to live in it. Upon her death in April 1902 she left $3000 to the Whittier Home Association for their projects, while the house was willed to her husband and son for their disposal or use.

4 Charles Harold Davis (1856–1933), Tonalist and Impressionist painter, was born in Amesbury, MA and studied in Paris, becoming one of the finest representatives of the Barbizon School.

5 "The Centennial Hymn" was written for the nation's Centennial Celebration in 1876, held in Philadelphia. The composer was a noted professor of music at Harvard. One newspaper account noted that the audience began applauding after the first line and continued throughout the whole singing of the piece.

6 Julia Ward Howe (1818–1910) was also noteworthy in the suffrage movement. Her son-in-law, John Elliot, began this painting in 1910, showing her at an earlier age. It was finished by Wm. Cotton in 1935. The oil on canvas portrait is used with permission from the National Portrait Gallery, The Smithsonian, Washington, DC.

7 Sanborn was one of the "Secret Six" along with Thomas Wentworth Higginson, Theodore Parker, Samuel Howe, Gerrit Smith, and George Luther Stearns. They supported and financed John Brown's antislavery efforts.

8 The editor has inserted subheadings in the addresses for clarity and ease of reading.

9 Whittier was colorblind.

10 This church was a Congregational church and is sometimes confused with the Old South (Presbyterian) Church on Federal Street where Rev. Whitefield was buried. It changed denominations around 1909 and was torn down circa 1940.

11 William Lloyd Garrison, Jr., was an anti-imperialist, opposed to the war with Spain, and advocated a single tax.

[12] Probably refers to the successes of Union blockades and Sherman's march through North and South Carolina leading to the imminent fall of the Confederacy.

[13] In 1842 an African American, George Latimer, was seized and jailed in Boston as requested by a man from Virginia who claimed to be his owner. For more details, see: http://myweb.northshore.edu/users/sherman/whittier/abolitionist/masstova.html.

[14] See http://www.assumption.edu/ahc/WhittierIchabod.html.
Roland Woodwell, in his biography of Whittier, describes an incident when the Hutchinson Family Singers sang this in a church in Fairfax, VA and faced having their permit to sing in Army camps revoked under instructions from General McClellan. Salmon P. Chase, Secretary of the Treasury, asked John Hutchinson for a copy of the poem. Woodwell writes,

> Two days later Chase told Hutchinson that the poem had been read at a Cabinet meeting, where it had met unanimous approval, and Lincoln had remarked that it was just the kind of song that he wanted the soldiers to hear and that Hutchinson might go among soldiers wherever they were invited to sing. Lincoln later told a Civil War correspondent that the reading of the poem had influenced him to issue the Emancipation Proclamation. See p. 303–304.

[15] Author Lydia Maria Francis Child was the center portrait in a group of seven women prominent in the suffrage and women's rights movements. Created and published by L. Prang & Co., c. 1870. Courtesy of Library of Congress.

[16] Lucretia Mott, a liberal Quaker, helped found Philadelphia's Female Anti-Slavery Society and was a suffragette with Elizabeth Cady Stanton. Portrait used with permission from the National Portrait Gallery, The Smithsonian, Washington, DC.

[17] This statue of the speaker's father was created by Daniel Chester French and erected in Brown Square, Newburyport, MA July 4, 1893.

[18] Woodman's reminiscences used with permission by the Haverhill Public Library, Whittier Collection.

[19] Postcard of the Page House circa 1910 used with permission of the Danvers Historical Society.

[20] *The Significance of Being Frank* by Tom Foran Clark, April 2007, an E-book biography http://www.bungalowshop.com/sanborn/index.html.

[21] Sanborn's address is reprinted with permission of the Salem Public Library.

[22] Illustrations of Henry Clay, Lowell Mills, Ralph Waldo Emerson, John Brown, Harper's Ferry, and Thomas Higginson courtesy of the Library of Congress.

[23] Sanborn gave this additional information in his speech:

"...it is a curious fact that a younger brother of the Kansas hero John Brown continued to be an active partisan of Clay, and edited a New Orleans newspaper in his interest, during the first administration of Jackson, and until his own death in 1833. Of his own son, Salmon Brown, his father, the old Calvinist Owen Brown, said years afterward: 'Salmon was of some note a gentleman. But I never knew that he gave evidence of being a Christian.'"

WHITTIER RESOURCES AND RECOMMENDED READING

Freeman, Donald C., John "Ben" Pickard and Roland H. Woodwell. *Whittier and Whittierland: Portrait of a Poet and His World*. Haverhill, MA: *Trustees of the Whittier Homestead, 1976*.

Jolliff, William, ed., *The Poetry of John Greenleaf Whittier, A Reader's Edition*, Richmond, IN: Friends United Press, 2000.

Pickard, John "Ben," *A House Becomes a Home — The Women of the Amesbury Whittier House; Whittier as a Local Poet;* and *Whittier and his Elizabeths*, Amesbury, MA 2007.

Pickard, Samuel T., *Whittier-Land: A Handbook of North Essex*, Cambridge, MA: The Riverside Press, 1904.

Smith, Emily Binney, *Whittier*. Amesbury, MA: The Whittier Press, 1935.

Wineapple, Brenda, ed., *John Greenleaf Whittier: Selected Poems*, American Poets Project, New York: NY, The Library of America, 2004.

Woodwell, Roland H., *John Greenleaf Whittier: A Biography*, Haverhill, MA; Published under the auspices of The Trustees of the John Greenleaf Whittier Homestead, 1985.

Wright, Donald Prescott. ed. *John Greenleaf Whittier, A Profile in Pictures*, Haverhill, MA: Published under the auspices of The Trustees of the John Greenleaf Whittier Homestead, 1967.

Local Websites

Whittier Home Association: www.whittierhome.org

John Greenleaf Whittier Homestead www.johngreenleafwhittier.com

Essex County's Famous Son: www.whittierpoetry.org

APPENDIX

ACKNOWLEDGMENTS

I was fortunate to have so many local resources for this Whittier Bicentennial project. Whittier's definitive biography, published in 1985, was written by Roland Woodwell, an English teacher at Amesbury High School from 1923 to 1966. Those of us who were fortunate to have been his students when he was chairman of the English Department knew he had spent decades researching Whittier.

More importantly, Woodwell's biography brings Whittier to general readers, not just scholars. At first one dips in and out of this "tome" looking for specific facts, but then realizes that he's telling such a marvelous story, one really needs to start at the beginning. This book provided a strong foundation for the Whittier Home Association and especially the Exhibit Committee.

I could not begin to research this topic had it not been for the women of the Whittier Home Association, who began keeping records and making scrapbooks chronicling their programs, work, and interests more than one hundred years ago. Stephanie Caverno, site manager, shared these and other valuable resources with me. One document with personal interest was the Whittier Home Association 1898 membership list, which included, to my surprise, my great-great-grand-mother's name.

Many institutions also shared their material. One vital resource was the Haverhill Public Library. I am particularly indebted to Interim Director Mary Johnson-Lally and Jennifer Lyon, for their interest, support, and extraordinary help retrieving and copying invaluable documents from the Special Collections. The Portrait Gallery of the Smithsonian Institution, Houghton Library of Harvard University, Smith College, Peabody Essex Museum, Salem Public Library, Danvers Historical Society, and Whittier Homestead Trustees also kindly gave permission to reproduce related documents. Thanks also to Susan Herman who shared her work while developing the Whittier poetry website hosted by Northshore Community College.

John "Ben" Pickard, Whittier scholar, read an early draft of the manuscript and generously shared his enthusiasm, anecdotes, family scrapbooks, and editorial wisdom. He is truly a friend of the Whittier Home Association and Amesbury.

I appreciate the support and interest of my fellow members of the Exhibit Committee. Meeting monthly for two years, we've shared our ideas, sources, progress, and road trips right from the beginning—truly a community of learning. I am grateful to Janet Howell, our chair and current Board president, for creating this committee and last year suggesting that I write about my chosen topic.

—Pamela Johnson Fenner, 2007, Amesbury, MA.

THE WHITTIER HOME
BICENTENNIAL EXHIBIT COMMITTEE

Recognizing that December 17, 2007 would be the 200th anniversary of Whittier's birth, the Board of Directors of the Whittier Home Association voted in 2005 to form an Exhibit Committee. This group of willing members, led by Chair Janet Howell, would study the life of Whittier, explore his legacy, research an individual topic of our choosing, and learn how to put on a professional museum exhibit.

Janet and grant-writer/project curator, Carolyn Singer, successfully raised funds—local, state, national, and private—to make it possible to have many educational opportunities. The first was a three-day workshop with Jane Lancaster teaching about women in nineteenth-century New England and Joanne Pope Melish teaching about slavery in New England. That was followed by a day-long workshop on exhibit design and one on labeling.

Next we focused on how to do a historic house interpretation. We began a 1-½ day workshop with scholars from all over the country who were experts in the areas of Whittier's life we had chosen. From that session, we chose five themes that we would use to interpret the Whittier Home:

- **Moral**: His Quaker beliefs informed his ideas on equality of race, gender, and class.
- **Hardship**: He overcame poverty and a meager education and attainedboth prominence and financial security.
- **Home Life**: His New England roots, nature, and strong family ties nourished him and shaped his identity.
- **Soulmate**: His relationship with his sister, also a published writer, inspired him.
- **Paradoxes**:
    - He was a pacifist, but supported the Civil War.
    - He became a politician and national figure although by nature he was solitary.
    - Despite his high regard for women, he never married.

The group visited seven historic house museums: The Mount (Edith Wharton), The Evergreens (Emily Dickinson), The Manse (Nathaniel Hawthorne), Orchard House (The Alcotts), and the homes of Ralph Waldo Emerson,

Henry Wadsworth Longfellow (Portland, ME), and Sarah Orne Jewett. Following each house visit, we evaluated the institution in terms of themes and tour expertise.

The fall and early winter of 2006 were spent preparing the community-wide exhibits for the May 2007 opening. Additional funding through grants and community donations made it possible to execute the plans. The group found it an amazing experience and hope to continue with more research projects together.

Joanne Melish and Jane Lancaster lead workshop

EXHIBIT COMMITTEE AND RESEARCH TOPICS

Nan Becker — *The Burning of Pennsylvania Hall*

Elly Becotte — *Folklore and Legends*

Sue Curry and Rosemary Rodie
The WHA Gardens and "Summer Kitchen"

Pamela Fenner — *The Whittier Centennial (1907)*

Harriet Gould — *Whittier's Early Life*
The Influence of the Farm and Family on his Values

Maureen Leahy — *The Whittier Home*

Donna Titus, Julia Faulkner, and Margaret Nichols
Women in Whittier's Life

Annie Tunstall — *The Influence of the Quaker Religion*

WHITTIER'S AUTOBIOGRAPHY, IN LETTER FORM

Amesbury, 5th Mo., 1882

Dear Friend :—I am asked in thy note of this morning to give some account of my life. There is very little to give. I can say with Canning's knife-grinder: "Story, God bless you! I have none to tell you!"

I was born on the 17th of December, 1807, in the easterly part of Haverhill, Mass., in the house built by my first American ancestor, two hundred years ago. My father was a farmer, in moderate circumstances,—a man of good natural ability, and sound judgment. For a great many years he was one of the Selectmen of the town, and was often called upon to act as arbitrator in matters at issue between neighbors. My mother was Abigail Hussey, of Rollinsford, NH. A bachelor uncle and a maiden aunt, both of whom I remember with much affection, lived in the family. The farm was not a very profitable one; it was burdened with debt and we had no spare money; but with strict economy we lived comfortably and respectably. Both my parents were members of the Society of Friends. I had a brother and two sisters. Our home was somewhat lonely, half hidden in oak woods, with no house in sight, and we had few companions of our age, and few occasions of recreation. Our school was only for twelve weeks in a year,— in the depth of winter, and half a mile distant. At an early age I was set at work on the farm, and doing errands for my mother, who, in addition to her ordinary house duties, was busy in spinning and weaving the linen and woolen cloth needed in the family. On First-days, father and mother, and sometimes one of the children, rode down to the Friends' Meeting-house in Amesbury, eight miles distant. I think I rather enjoyed staying at home and wandering in the woods, or climbing Job's hill, which rose abruptly from the brook which rippled down at the foot of our garden. From the top of the hill I could see the blue outline of the Deerfield mountains in New Hampshire, and the solitary peak of Agamenticus on the coast of Maine. A curving line of morning mist marked the course of the Merrimac, and Great Pond, or Kenoza, stretched away from the foot of the hill towards the village of Haverhill hidden from sight by intervening hills and woods, but which sent to us the sound of its two church bells. We had only about twenty volumes of books, most of them the journals of pioneer ministers in our society. Our only annual was an almanac. I was early fond of reading, and now and then heard of a book of biography or travel, and walked miles to borrow it.

When I was fourteen years old my first school-master, Joshua Coffin, the able, eccentric historian of Newbury, brought with him to our house a volume of Burns' poems, from which he read, greatly to my delight. I begged him to leave the book with me; and set myself at once to the task of mastering the glossary of the Scottish dialect at its close. This was about the first poetry I had ever read (with the exception of that of the Bible, of which I had been a close student), and it had a lasting influence upon me. I began to make rhymes myself, and to imagine stories and adventures. In fact I lived a sort of dual life, and in a world of fancy, as well as in the world of plain matter-of-fact about me. My father always had a weekly newspaper, and when young Garrison started his "Free Press" at Newburyport, he took it in the place of the 'Haverhill Gazette." My sister, who was two years older than myself, sent one of my poetical attempts to the editor. Some weeks afterwards the news-carrier came along on horse-back and threw the paper out from his saddle-bags. My uncle and I were mending fences. I took up the sheet, and was surprised and overjoyed to see my lines in the "Poet's Corner." I stood gazing at them in wonder, and my uncle had to call me several times to my work before I could recover myself. Soon after, Garrison came to our farm-house, and I was called in from hoeing in the corn-field to see him. He encouraged me, and urged my father to send me to school. I longed for education, but the means to procure it were wanting. Luckily, the young man who worked for us on the farm in summer, eked out his small income by making ladies' shoes and slippers in the winter; and I learned enough of him to earn a sum sufficient to carry me through a term of six months in the Haverhill Academy. The next winter I ventured upon another expedient for raising money, and kept a district school in the adjoining town of Amesbury, thereby enabling me to have another academy term. The next winter I spent in Boston, writing for a paper. Returning in the spring, while at work on the farm, I was surprised by an invitation to take charge of the Hartford (Ct.) "Review," in the place of the famous George D. Prentice, who had removed to Kentucky. I had sent him some of my school "compositions," which he had received favorably. I was unwilling to lose the chance of doing something more in accordance with my taste, and, though I felt my unfitness for the place, I accepted it, and remained nearly two years, when I was called home by the illness of my father, who died soon after. I then took charge of the farm, and worked hard to "make both ends meet;" and, aided by my mother's and sister's thrift and economy, in some measure succeeded.

As a member of the Society of Friends, I had been educated to regard Slavery as a great and dangerous evil, and my sympathies were strongly enlisted for the oppressed slaves by my intimate acquaintance with William Lloyd Garrison.

When the latter started his paper in Vermont, in 1828, I wrote him a letter commending his views upon Slavery, Intemperance, and War, and assuring him that he was destined to do great things. In 1833 I was a delegate to the first National Anti-Slavery Convention, at Philadelphia. I was one of the Secretaries of the Convention and signed its Declaration. In 1833 I was in the Massachusetts Legislature. I was mobbed in Concord, N. H., in company with George Thompson, afterwards member of the British Parliament, and narrowly escaped from great danger. I kept Thompson, whose life was hunted for, concealed in our lonely farm-house for two weeks. I was in Boston during the great mob in Washington Street, soon after, and was threatened with personal violence.

In 1837 I was in New York, in conjunction with Henry B. Stanton and Theodore D. Weld, in the office of the American Anti-Slavery Society. The next year I took charge of the "Pennsylvania Freeman," an organ of the Anti-Slavery Society. My office was sacked and burned by a mob soon after, but I continued my paper until my health failed, when I returned to Massachusetts. The farm in Haverhill had, in the meantime, been sold, and my mother, aunt, and youngest sister had moved to Amesbury, near the Friends' Meeting-house, and I took up my residence with them. All this time I had been actively engaged in writing for the anti-slavery cause. In 1833 I printed at my own expense an edition of my first pamphlet, "Justice and Expediency." With the exception of a few dollars from the "Democratic Review" and "Buckingham's Magazine," I received nothing for my poems and literary articles. Indeed, my pronounced views on Slavery made my name too unpopular for a publisher's uses. I edited in 1844 the "Middlesex Standard," and afterwards became associate editor of the "National Era," at Washington. I early saw the necessity of separate political action on the part of Abolitionists. And was one of the founders of the Liberty Party—the germ of the present Republican Party.

Whittier portrait at
Whittier Home Association

In 1837 an edition of my complete poems, up to that time, was published by Ticknor & Fields. "In War Time," followed in 1864, and in 1863, "Snow-bound." In 1860 I was chosen a member of the Electoral College of Massachusetts, and also in 1864. I have been a member of the Board of Overseers of Harvard College, and a Trustee of Brown University. But while feeling, and willing to meet, all the responsibilities of citizenship, and deeply interested in questions which concern the welfare and honor of the country, I have, as a rule, declined overtures for acceptance of public stations. I have always taken an active part in elections, but have not been willing to add my own example to the greed of office.

I have been a member of the Society of Friends by birth-right, and by a settled conviction of the truth of its principles and the importance of its testimonies, while, at the same time, I have a kind feeling towards all who are seeking, in different ways from mine, to serve God and benefit their fellow-men.

Neither of my sisters are living. My dear mother, to whom I own much every way, died in 1858. My brother is still living, in the city of Boston. My niece, his daughter, who was with me for some years, is now the wife of S. T. Pickard, Esq., of Portland, Maine. Since she left me I have spent much of my time with esteemed relatives at Oak Knoll, Danvers, Mass., though I still keep my homestead at Amesbury, where I am a voter.

My health was never robust; I inherited from both my parents a sensitive, nervous temperament; and one of my earliest recollections is of pain in the head, from which I have suffered all my life. For many years I have not been able to read or write for more than half an hour at a time; often not so long. Of late, my hearing has been defective. But in many ways I have been blest far beyond my deserving; and, grateful to the Divine Providence, I tranquilly await the close of a life which has been longer, and on the whole happier, than I had reason to expect, although far different from that which I dreamed of in youth. My experience confirms the words of old time, that "it is not in man who walketh to direct his steps." Claiming no exemption from the sins and follies of our common humanity, I dare not complain of their inevitable penalties. I have had to learn renunciation and submission, and

> "Knowing
> That kindly Providence its care is showing
> In the withdrawal as in the bestowing, Scarcely I dare for more or less
> to pray."

Thy friend,

JOHN G. WHITTIER

CHILDREN IN THE AMESBURY
CENTENNIAL CHORUS

Edna Aldrich
John Ashley
Eleanor Attchison
Arline Avery
Chester Bailey
Ruth Baker
Edith Barteau
Irene Barteau
Lois Bartlett
Burll Beers
Cyril Bishop
Harold Blake
Jessie Blake
Raymond Blake
Rena Blake
Roland Blake
Harely Brown
Marguerite Burbank
Hazel Burrill
Annie Caie
Arthur Caie
Arthur Chase
Edward Chesley
Louise Chesley
Certrude Chrowe
Gertrude Cole
Eugene Collins
Harold Congdon
Augusta Davis
Hannah Dow
Lyle Drew
Olve Fellows
Ethel Fiske
Mary French
Helen Fuller

Leroy Goddard
Henry Goodale
May Goodale
William Goodwin
Herbert Gray
Eva Graves
Fanny Gurney
Sila Hansen
Elsie Hatch
Grace Hatch
Annie Henson
Hermeline Hiron
Antoinette Houle
Frankie Hunt
Josie Inglis
Lillian Inglis
Lida Kennedy
Leslie Kenenett
Ruth Kimball
Esther Lamprey
Lillian Lamprey
Josie Lane
Edith Locke
Jessie Locke
Laura Loud
Eileen MacLean
Elias MacLean
Robert McKenzie
Alice Lovering
Doris McNeil
Alice Miller
Ruth Miller
Henrietta Parkman
Sadie Parson
Unabell Pettengill

Roy Pousland
Ruth Prescott
Elizabeth Pride
Harold Proctor
Emma Randall
Ida Randall
Maud Randall
Gertrude Roell
Raymond Sanborn
Warren Sanborn
Godfrey Scott
Blanche Scribner
Asa Shaw
Ruth Sheefe
Ruth Swett
Wilbur Swett
Wealey Tobey
Howard Todd
Dan Trombla
Alice True
Ruby Tuxbury
Chester Vaillancourt
Florence Vaillancourt
Edna Varrells
Arlene Walker
Bertha Wilbur
Almeda Wilson
Frances Wilson
Bertie Woodward
Charles Woodward
Harry Woodward
Rhena Woodward

NOTABLE GUESTS AT THE
AMESBURY CENTENNIAL

Mrs. S. A. Addison
Mrs. Thomas Bailey Aldrich, Boston
Mr. & Mrs. Talbot Aldrich
Margaret H. Aubin
Mrs. Frederick B. Ayer, Lowell
Mrs. Louis Barnes, Methuen
Mrs. William Bartlett, Boston
Henry B. Blackwell
Alice Stone Blackwell
Miss A. Lincoln Bowls
Miss M. H. Bridgman
Mrs. Brown, Portsmouth
Philip A. Burton
Mr. & Mrs. Philip Butler, Auburndale
Miss Carrie Carter, Haverhill
Mrs. Gertrude Whittier Cartland
Miss Carrie Cate
Lucy Chase
Sarah Chase
Allen Coffin, Nantucket
Dr. Samuel E. Courtney, Boston
Charles Cowley, Lowell
Mrs. Richard H. Dana
Mrs. George Danforth
Miss Susan Isabelle Downs, Boston
Elizabeth P. Dunham
Misses Emory, Newburyport
George S. Fiske
Sam Walter Foss, Somerville
Mr. & Mrs. Jones Frankle, Haverhill
Mrs. Charles Fredick, Portsmouth
Francis J. Garrison
William Lloyd Garrison, [Jr.]
George E. Gilchrist
H. M. Gove, Waltham
Mrs. Sarah Abbey Gove
William Carroll Hill, Boston
Mrs. R. Holman, Nashua, NH
Mrs. Harry Hovey, Portsmouth, NH

Mrs. Horace Hovey, Newburyport
James A. Howe
Mrs. Allan Hudson, Brockton
Mr. & Mrs. James Hussey, Portland, ME
Miss Sarah Orne Jewett, Boston
Augustine Jones, Newton, MA
Mr. & Mrs. Nathaniel N. Jones,
    Newburyport
Harriet McCuen Kimball, Portsmouth
Henry T. Kitson
Mrs. Theo. A. Ruggles Kitson
Mrs. Francis W. Kittredge, Boston
Mrs. Harriet Minot Laughlin
Ex-Governor John J. Long, Boston
Miss Alice Longfellow, Cambridge
Mrs. Stephen Lowe, Boston
Miss Adeline Mann
Miss Adeline May
Edward F. May
Lucia Ames Mead
Miss A. Marion Merrill, Somerville
Miss Frances Mills, Mt. Vernon, IA
Mrs. Charles Mitchell, Boston
Mrs. Clement A. Morgan
Miss L. Nelson
Mrs. W. H. Niles, Lynn
Mrs. E. Norcross
Mrs. John Noyes, Boston
Miss Mary Noyes, Boston
Mrs. Marion Longfellow O'Donoghue,
    Cambridge
Mrs. O'Neil, Boston
Mary H. Perkins
Charles I. Pettingell
Samuel L. Porter
Mrs. Purrington, Boston
John Ritchie, Boston
Mrs. Rollins, Newburyport
Mrs. Herbert Sawyer

Mrs. A. Wright Sewell, Cambridge
Miss Fanny Sparhawk, Newton Center
Cornelia P. Stone
Major John W. Stott, Lowell
Mrs. William C. Tapan, Hyde Park
Mr. William Thayer, Cambridge
Mrs. J. G. Thorp
Mrs. Charles Tredick, Portsmouth
Mr. George Fox Tucker, Boston
Mrs. Mary E. Tufts
Herbert S. Ward, Newton Centre

Dr. Booker T. Washington, Tuskegee
A. C. Webster
Miss Sarah Greenleaf Weeden, Boston
Mrs. Alden P. White, Salem
William F. Whittemore
Frank W. Whittier
Miss Whittier, Boston
Mrs. Charles W. Whittier
Miss Jane Wood, Newburyport
Mrs. Ida Vose Woodbury, Boston

GUESTS ON THE STAGE AT THE TOWN HALL
AMESBURY CENTENNIAL

Col. Edwin W. M. Bailey
Samuel. R. Bailey
George Birdseye
Judge Henry S. Braley
G. Cammett
Hon. George W. Cate
Jacob Choate
Seth Clark
Dr. Samuel E. Courtney
Charles Cowley
Hon. Davis Cross
John James Currier
J. Albert Davis
Mr. William Dewhurst
Dr. J. A. Douglass
A. J. Felden
H. H. Fielden
Jones Frankle
W. E. Fuller
William Lloyd Garrison [Jr.]
Hon. E. B. George
Hon. Williard J. Hale
James Hassett
William W. Hawkes
A. C. Hill
James Hume

J. R. Huntington
James Hussey
Col. Samuel A. Johnson
Mr. Francis W. Kittredge
Ex-Governor John D. Long
Hon. Jere. T. Mahoney
D. C. Maxfield
Edwin D. Mead
F. W. Merrill
Charles Mitchell
William A. Murphy
Hon. Wm. H. Niles
John Noyes
Dr. Robert E. Park
Samuel T. Pickard
A. W. Reddy
Mr. John Riccard
Judge James B. Richardson
Edward Rowell
Rep. Porter Sargent
H. A. Sawyer
Judge Edgar J. Sherman, Boston,
    Representing the Commonwealth
Mrs. Emily Binney Smith
Mr. George Fox Tucker
Herbert S. Ward

Dr. Booker T. Washington
A. C. Webster
Hon. Alden P. White
Charles Whittier

=================================

Rev. Mr. Barker
Rev. Robert W. Beers, Somerville
Rev. E. P. Constant
Rev. W. J. Dawson
Rev. James Dingwell
Rev. Dix
Rev. Dr. A. E. Dunning
Rev. Albert P. Fitch
Rev. George A. Gordon
Rev. George. H. Gutterson, Boston
Rev. Chauncey J. Hawkins
Rev. Charles Sumner Holton
Rev. Dr. Hovey
Rev. Allen Hudson, Brockton
Rev. Frank S. Hunnewell
Rev. William Allen Knight
Rev. Robert Le B. Lynch
Rev. Herbert A. Manchester
Rev. Mr. McCrone
Rev. Dr. W. T. McElveen
Rev. Mr. Nilan
Rev. James E. Norcross
Rev. E. Norcross
Rev. A. M. Osgood
Rev. H. Grant Person
Rev. William C. Rand
Rev. William H. Ryder
Rev. John L. Sewall
Rev. Allan Stockdale
Rev. Dr. Thayer
Rev. Francis Tiffany
Rev. Mr. Wilson
Rev. William Allen Wright
—and others

110

Description of the history of the Friends' Meetinghouse in Amesbury, their several locations and the improvements of the present building up until the Whittier Centennial

The Friends' Meetinghouse.

Among the attractions which Amesbury offers those who make the pilgrimage to the Whittier land, next to the modest home on Friend street, where the poet did his life work, is the Friends' Meeting House, and many enter the church and take a seat in the Whittier pew as though they were treading on holy ground.

And here in its accustomed place
I look on memory's dearest face;
The blind by-sitter guesseth not
What shadow haunts that vacant spot;
No eye save mine alone can see,
The love wherewith it welcomes me.

Thus did the poet express the emotion which controlled him while attending worship, and it is a feeling akin to this that takes possession of those who in fancy see the poet when they enter the old church.

The first Friends' meeting house in Amesbury was located not far from the site of No. 8 mill of the Hamilton Woolen Co., on the bank of the Powow river, and was built in 1705. In fact, it was a log cabin. The building of this meeting house was an important event in the history of the Friends, and required much deliberation on the part of those at Hampton, N. H., where for the previous four years the Amesbury Friends had worshipped.

According to tradition, there was a church built between the one in 1705 and that of 1903, and while the site is unknown, it is believed to have been near that of the first one.

In 1808 it was decided to build a new house of worship, which was located where the Church of the Sacred Heart now stands. It was to this church that the Whittier family went on first coming to Amesbury, and the poet soon became one of its most influential members.

That the associations of this place must have bee nsuch as to have caused them regret in leavinfi, it is certain as the church was surrounded by the cemetery in which many who had passed on were sleeping the last sleep, but in 1849 the quietness that was wanted in their meetings was disturbed by the nearness of houses and it was decided to sell and seek a new location.

The old church was sold to the Free Baptist Society, that had just been organized and the old building was moved to Pond street, where it is now used as a tenement house, the only change being the addition of bay windows, new windows and an "L," and until a few years ago the same doors were doing duty.

The present meeting house was built in 1850 and the details of construction were left to the poet Whittier.

The late Mrs. S. T. Pickard, who was the poet's niece, in speaking of the building of the present church by he runcle, at the celebration of his birthday in 1901, said:

"Some of the Friends feared he would be too modern in his ideas and add unnecessary comforts, but when he employed three elderly carpenters all members of the Friends Society their fears vanished, and the result was the very plain house which has now become famous because it was where he worshipped."

Some 20 years ago the interior was remodelled and new oak pews substituted for the old ones in half of the church; a furnace was placed in the basement and the floor was carpeted, but the original lines of the building were preserved, an dthe elder's seat in front and the sliding division through the center of the building, by which the room can be made into two, remain the same as in the original building.

Some eight years ago the other half of the interior was improved and today the church is quite modern in its appearance. The division not only reduced the size of the room, but originally the lower half was used as the dividing line between the men and the women, and when any important matter was to come before the elders, the subject could be considered by the men and women separately.

When the smaller room was used, the men sat on one side of an aisle and the women on the other, but this custom has been done away with and the seating is the same as in other churches, but the elders and elderesses still occupy the seat in front.

When Whittier rst moved to Amesbury, no one took part in the meetings unless "moved by the spirit" to do so, and meetings where they would sit for an hour without a word being spoken were the rule rather than the exception.

This was the kind of a meeting that the poet enjoyed, as he often remarked that "a prayer and quiet meditatio nis what I call a good meeting."

The church has no organ and what singing there was in the olden time was "as the spirit moved." On one occasion a woman spoke and sung in the meeting more after the style of an evangelist, and the poet remarked to a friend: "I didn't know as we would ever be able to get the sing out of the meeting house."

Special Whittier Centennial Edition
The Amesbury Daily News

ABOUT THE EDITOR

Pamela Johnson Fenner grew up in Amesbury, MA and attended the local public schools. Her interest in history began when her family explored old New England cemeteries. Her earliest connection to the name "Whittier" was during her childhood watching her mother make tea sandwiches for monthly Whittier Home Association meetings. Later, she followed the construction of the Whittier Bridge over the Merrimac River and participated in its dedication. Roland Woodwell, Whittier's biographer, was her high school English teacher.

She completed a BS in Biology from Chatham College a Master of Arts in Teaching (MAT-Natural Science) from Harvard University, and a Waldorf teacher education program at Rudolf Steiner College.

While living in northern California, Pam launched Michaelmas Press to publish education and parenting books. Her previous publishing experience had been as a reporter and later Editor of the High School Page at *The Amesbury Daily News*.

Returning to Amesbury in 1995, she joined the Whittier Home Association serving on the Board of Directors from 2002–06 and its President from 2004–06. In addition, Pam is a member of the Haverhill Whittier Club, Amesbury Treasures, Newburyport Choral Society, Independent Publishers of New England (IPNE), and the Amesbury Chamber of Commerce.

Celebrating Whittier is her fifth title and the first in a history genre. Her previous book was *Books for the Journey,* a high school reading list. A mother of three daughters, she enjoys gardening with her husband, Paul, and is working on her next book, an elementary school reading list.

INDEX

Garrison, Francis J., 9, 108
Garrison, William Lloyd, 22, 43, 44, 47, 48, 54, 55, 62, 63, 92, 104
Garrison, Jr., William Lloyd, 35, 37, 43-55, 95, 109
George, Hon. E. B., 109
George, Mrs. G. W., 7
Gilchrist, George E., 108
Goethe, Johann Wolfgang von, 91
Gordon, Rev., George A., 110
Gould, Harriet, 102
Gove, Edward, 62
Gove, H. M., 108
Gove, Mrs. A. N., 7
Gove, Sarah Abbey, 108
Gray, Thomas, 62
Great Britain, 69
Great Pond, 103
Greenland, Henry, 62, 64
Grimke sisters, 49
Guardian, The, 78
Guimant, 25
Gutterson, Rev. Dr. George, 110
Hague, The, Netherlands, 33
Hale, Hon. Williard J., 109
Halstead, Hon. Murat, 9
Hampton Institute, 14, 15
Hancock, John, 54
Hanson, Miss Harriet, 66
"Harp at Nature's advent strong, The," 36
Harper, John Adams, 70
Harper's Ferry, 51, 75, 96
Hartford, CT, 22, 46, 63, 66
Harvard College, 68, 80, 95, 105, 111
Hassett, James H., 8, 18, 109
Haverhill Academy, 104
Haverhill Historical Society, 30
Haverhill Public Library, 30, 96, 100
Haverhill Whittier Club, 23
Hawkes, Mrs. William W., 7
Hawkes, William W., 18, 109
Hawkins, Rev. Chauncey J., 110
Hawley, 36

Hawthorne, Mrs. Nathaniel, 66
Hawthorne, Nathaniel, 2, 59, 66
Hay, Hon. John, 9
Hayes, John Russell, 93
Henry, Patrick, 54
Herald of Freedom, 67
Higginson, Thomas Wentworth, 39, 78, 79, 92, 96
Hill, A. C., 109
Hill, James W., 25
Hill, Mrs. S., 7
Hill, William Carroll, 108
Hines, Ezra D., 59
Historical Society of Old Newbury, 35, 38, 40
History of Haverhill, 1823, 83
Hoar, Hon. George F., 9
Holland, 61
Holman, Mrs. R., 108
Holmes, Oliver Wendell, 45
Homestead [*See also* Birthplace], 21-23, 97, 106
Holton, Rev. Charles Sumner, 110
"Hope of the Ages," 37
Horton, Mrs. A. M., 7
Hotel Somerset, 82
Houghton, Mifflin and Co., 83
Hovey, Mrs. Harry, 108
Hovey, Mrs. Horace, 108
Hovey, Rev. Dr., 110
Howarth, Mrs. J. H., 7
Howarth, Mrs. John H., 8
Howe, Dean, 10
Howe, Dr. Samuel Gridley, 68
Howe, James A., 108
Howe, Julia Ward, 23-26, 29, 95
Howell, Janet, 100, 101
Hoyt, Mrs. F. M., 7
Hudson, Rev. Allen, 110
Hudson, Mrs. Allen, 108
Huguenot Greenleaf, 44
Hume, Elizabeth, 7
Hume, James, 9, 109

Publications listed in the Whittier Resources and
Recommended Reading are available at the
Whittier Home Association Gift Shop
86 Friend Street
PO Box 632
Amesbury, MA 01913

978-388-1337
www.whittierhome.org

For information about special sales, volume
discounts of this and other titles contact:

Michaelmas Press
PO Box 702
Amesbury, MA 01913

978-388-7066

Website: www.michaelmaspress.com
Email: pam@michaelmaspress.com
pjfenner@mac.com